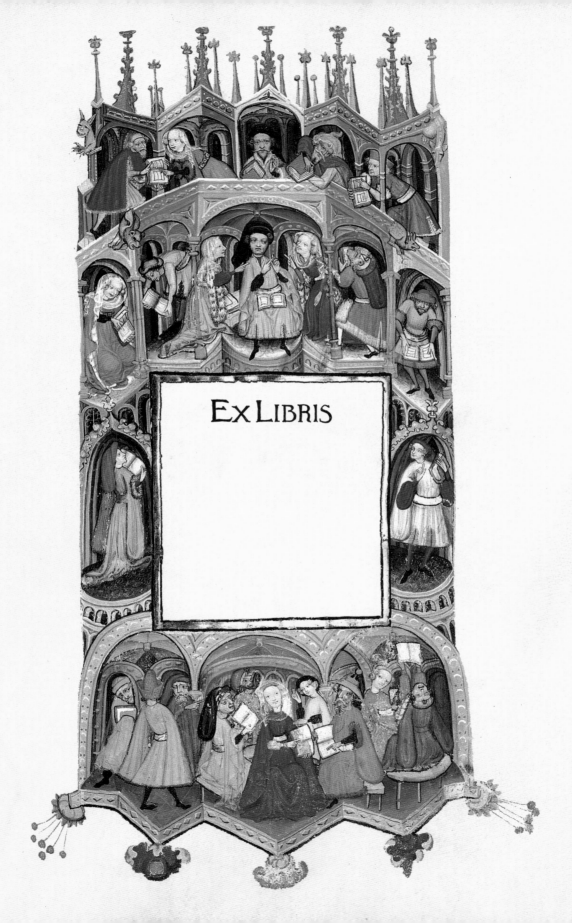

EX LIBRIS

A
MEDIEVAL
MISCELLANY

SELECTED AND EDITED BY
JUDITH HERRIN

MANUSCRIPT SELECTION AND BOOK DESIGN BY
LINDA & MICHAEL FALTER

WITH AN INTRODUCTION BY
EMMANUEL LE ROY LADURIE

WEIDENFELD & NICOLSON
FACSIMILE EDITIONS

Contents

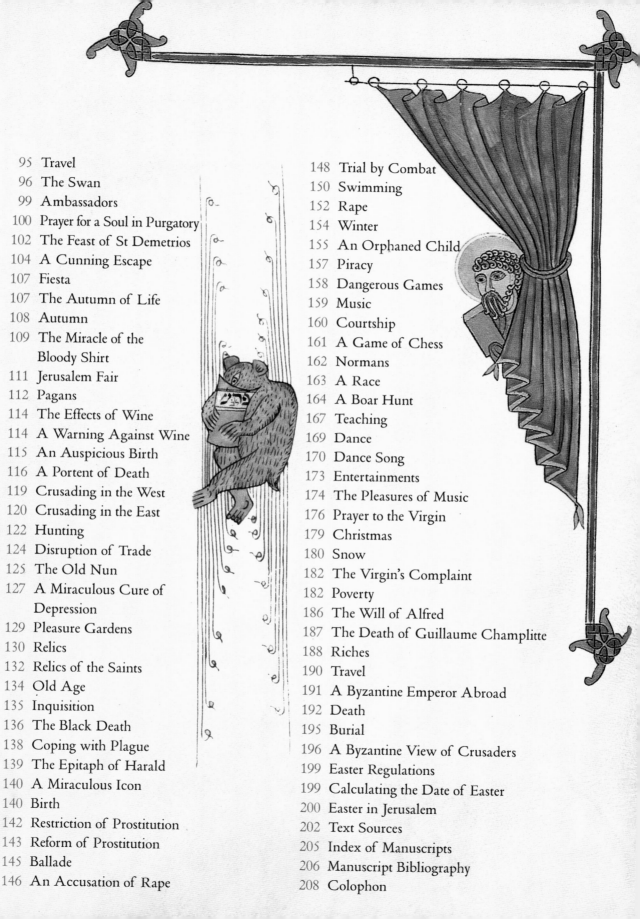

Introduction

Before introducing these dazzling texts, selected with great skill by Judith Herrin, perhaps I may outline the possible content of this type of medieval miscellany. I take as my starting point Georges Dumézil's general theory of the three functions, also favoured by the great French scholars Georges Duby and Jacques Le Goff. This theory allows me to give you an overview of the basic medieval landscape, as it is illustrated by this rich study of the Middle Ages.

The three functions: priests, soldiers and peasants (*oratores, bellatores, aratores*), or, broadly speaking the fields of church and state (sovereignty); of battle and nobility; and the field, both in the literal and metaphorical sense, of fertility. Though the word is redolent of the pastoral and agricultural, it extends to all that is fecund, including the leading role of woman in giving birth to children ⁄ and more generally in reproducing society. The offices of those who pray, those who fight and those who produce and reproduce: were these (as a simplistic reading of Dumézil might suggest) the legacy of our Indo⁄European 'ancestors'? Or did they spring from the tripartite mentality of the Celts and the Germans, who are, in their turn, distant cousins of the Anglo⁄Saxons; or ⁄ in the final analysis (what a surprise!) ⁄ would they be a legacy of biblical tradition? In the Book of Genesis, an *angel*, armed with a *sword*, expels from the *verdant* paradise the *fecund* Eve; is this not trifunctional? Duby and Le Goff mention occasionally these ultimately muddled hypotheses, but are more interested in the development of the famous 'triplet' during the Middle Ages.

The stories, people and events recounted here are peppered with elements that would be relished by those great medieval scholars. In that distant age, priests prayed long and hard, and this activity gave them a status comparable to that of monks, and enabled them to ask God for favours which would benefit society. The soldiers of the Middle Ages (especially from the twelfth century onwards) were mounted knights who carried the heavy swords of battle, very different from the ancient Gallo⁄Roman nobility, who had worn belts of office which assimilated them into the imperial bureaucracy of Emperor Constantine. The third element of the triplet, the medieval peasants, were the object of ill⁄deserved contempt, though a stratum of *laboratores* ⁄ skilled labourers, and rich farmers ⁄ raised themselves above the common herd. They were more like the craftsmen and merchants who lived in towns.

The *King* had the quasi⁄magical sovereignty of a crowned priest or of an independent bishop. But as Le Goff says, the King's main function, above all, was to bind the three functions together. In effect, he was finally responsible for anything that went wrong, and a useful scapegoat who might lose his head for the 'common good' (something which Louis XIV and Charles I discovered after the end of what we call the Middle Ages).

A few words about the rural base, the ground floor of this great medieval edifice, which features prominently in the *Miscellany*. For the most part, the country inhabitants who had been valued in the ancient world disappeared ⁄ culturally speaking, at least ⁄ from the Merovingian period onwards. Or more precisely they sank into a state which we may characterise as the Pejorative. The peasant of the fifth century became synonymous with *paganus* (pagan) in the terms of the late Roman Empire; or what the ancient Hebrews called a *goy,* and the Greeks *ethnikos*: in other words, an uneducated farmer. He was thought of as the type who prevents the destruction of pagan temples, which nonetheless are destined sooner or later to be replaced, of course, by churches of the true Christian faith. To writers of the post⁄ classical period, the peasant was no more than a brute, barely human, a monster with a human face: the sinner, the lecher, the drunk, the pauper, the rustic; in short, a Caliban who had not yet found his Shakespeare. Thus it is all the more interesting to note the appearance of the word *labourer* (*kulak* in the good sense of the term) with most positive and favourable connotations after the year 926. The beginning of a new era, which valued the management of fertility, such as the science of husbandry and agriculture, which is often demonstrated in the texts selected with such learning by Judith Herrin.

It took a lot longer for the sexual productivity ⸻ that is, fertility ⸻ of women to be perceived as 'good' (and not only of those women who worked in the fields). As early as the third century, Clement of Alexandria had linked the sexual act to original sin, and St Augustine in turn nailed the problem between 395 and 430, asserting that lust was indeed the carrier of original sin, which thus became by definition sexually transmitted ⸻ a sort of metaphysical AIDS. The theory was not foolish; most civilisations have displayed a good dose of puritanism about what goes on 'down there'. Nonetheless, the consequences of St Augustine's writings were extensive and sometimes painful.

The second function concerns the weaponry ⸻ sharp and blunt ⸻ at the disposal of the 'aristos' and nobles, the trappings of a feudal system not to be confused with the tired image of feudalism handed down by post-'68 Marxist-Althusserians. The best medieval scholars view things as anthropologists or, better, as entomologists, observing the habits of red ants. They are interested above all in the gestures and the objects used in feudal acts of homage. Here is a world of allegory and parable; of image and figure: it defines a very particular symbolic system which is revealed in many features of this book. For example, the ceding of a fief (from lord to vassal), is symbolised by transference of simple objects: a stave of wood or a holly branch, a knife, a baton, an incense spoon; on another level, by a handshake, the contact of right thumbs or a kiss.

The third floor of our building houses religion ⸻ always closely allied to the political and power ⸻ and is well furnished. The primeval forest might be evoked in the pages that follow, but no longer as a sylvan link to labourers and peasants. To the intellectuals of the twelfth century, the woods were a place of renunciation, where monks and hermits withdrew from the world: the verdant equivalent of the sandy desert where the first anchorites of Sinai lived, or of that other 'desert' where the Camisards, persecuted Protestants of the eighteenth-century Cevennes, found a retreat, one well known to their English counterparts across the Channel. It also has an echo in the American Far West, where the 'horse whisperer' might seek refuge, far from the corruption of New York.

We thus firmly retie the triple braid of society, the finely interwoven strands of the trio of major functions; but we must also recognise other shared values ⸻ those represented, for example, by the serpent and the dragon in folk-tales which, despite the best efforts of the church, were still an integral part of urban life. Nor should we forget political history, often too quickly dismissed by historians of the *Annales* school when it is excessively narrative, but which they do not hesitate to use when assessing the ideological symbolism of the classic objects of power: the ring, the sceptre, the crown, the sword, the hand of justice and the red robes of the Chancellor of France…

II

Not surprisingly, religion takes pride of place in Judith Herrin's collection. In this realm of the sacred, pre-eminent in the Middle Ages, we learn first (and certainly not in alphabetical order) of Christ, of Augustinian theology and love of God; of the near-hysterical devotion of Catherine of Siena and of Margery Kempe; of the hereafter and of the Christian conversion of the Normans and Danes.

Miracles abound: those that tell of Christ's burial shroud, of abandoned children saved, of scholarly success, of the soul of a sinner imprisoned in a block of ice, or the supernatural lights of the Holy Sepulchre; even, the incredible severed head of St Genesius. Many document the cult of relics, which link mankind to heaven; tales of the 'music of the spheres', the fascination with famous sanctuaries and sacred cities, even when they are muddy; with processions and pilgrimages, which provided an outing for the Wife of Bath, and with the major feast days, beginning with Christmas. We should also mention other ways of going beyond the 'classic' devotion to religion: whether it involves total renunciation, individual combat with diabolical forces (the serpent Satan), or investigating other non-Christian elements of the miraculous, such as astrology.

The survey of political sovereignty (royal or imperial), inseparable from the realm of the supernatural but markedly Christian, is well documented here. It may reflect the 'model of models' - which is none other than a version of the Roman *imperium* with its magnetic qualities. Later King David appears (the model of Christian kingship); the spectacular *Basileus* in Byzantium; and Charlemagne, of course, swimming champion before Mao Tse-tung; then the Caliph of Baghdad and every western king, each with his long, long arm. Conflicts between kingdoms, and diplomatic links between England and Byzantium fall into the same category of the 'sacred ruler', which Jean Bodin would not have scorned. Similarly, the imperial court of Constantinople and the park of the Great Palace; the breaking of a seal as a symbol of the death of the one who held power while his successor waits to be enthroned; the inheritance of power by male heirs only (Salic Law before the letter); the game of chess as a political allegory *par excellence*. Also invoked are concepts such as Justice (by ordeal), Reason and its opponent Madness, Fortuna, Roman Liberty, the indispensable Education, even the sometimes smelly ruses employed by political leaders.

III

Herrin's collection contains fewer texts on the military and the nobility, but those there are, are excellent ('excellent fat' as Rabelais would have it). Here we assist at two falls of Constantinople, one in 1204, from inside the barricades, the other in 1453 when the Turkish artillery played its customary role in the final fall of Byzantium. The same for the capture of Antioch in 1098 and the conquest of England in 1066. Nor are strategies neglected: Pope

Urban II has much advice on this score, as does a Byzantine military commander, both sounding like the superannuated generals of today sagely making their idiotic comments. War, of course, is a beautiful daughter who becomes repellent, even when the Hungarians are defeated.

The warrior instincts of the nobility are treated, not directly but through aristocratic pastimes, in which they appear more or less explicitly. Hunting boar and big game, horse racing, and races between horses and warriors on foot (who often won); and carnival battles between Christian knights and others disguised as Moors.

IV

After the sacred and the violent, the third of our great functions is devoted to production and reproduction. The mention of agriculture means a discussion of the weather. At the turn of the millennium, this seems to have been warmer and milder than was later the case (in the 'little ice age' of the seventeenth century) and relations between medieval Europe and a temperate Greenland were 'alive and well'. But memories of harsh winters before the millennium feature in Herrin's pages, as well as blistering summers and grasshoppers! Autumn has a thousand glories heaped upon it by a Jewish author. Other articles are dedicated to the production of honey, to harvesting ⁄ the harvesters were struck by sunstroke ⁄ to threshing and more specifically to the Mediterranean style of 'dépiquage', very different from the threshing with rods practised in northern lands. Against this, there are few allusions to husbandry itself, apart from an article on shepherds. Wild beasts are represented by a bear, or rather by a bear⁄keeper of the seventh century.

The rural labourers I spoke of earlier find their incarnation in the figure (particularly puny, as it turns out) of Piers Plowman. There is a servant in our splendid string of texts but she is not a country girl but a laundress, a slave living in an urban environment. However, the singing of the *Magnificat* reminds us that whatever social differences divide us, we are all equal in the sight of God, in principle.

From agriculture and social concerns in general we pass to the world of commerce: fairs ⁄ English and Byzantine ⁄ negotiations with China, the crisis in the Mediterranean silk trade in 1118, importation of luxuries from Russia, Byzantium, Arabia and France.

But there are many other ways to make money, for the most part, illicit: piracy is the most important, especially on the Asian and Arab coasts; theft and minor rural delinquencies; racketeering by ferrymen and Basque brigands, and finally more 'innocent' ways through betting on games of dice. Material life (food and lodging) are treated in the case of a starving Norwegian and the shack of a poor woman set in the rich land of Flanders.

For human reproduction, Saint Artemios is the Asclepius of testicles and at the other end of the body, Saint Foy de Conques takes care of baldness. Birth can be dramatic as Guibert de Nogent recalls, and childhood seems to be more appreciated ⁄ even fondly remembered by some adults ⁄ than Philippe Ariès believed. As life progresses through youth and adolescence, love takes the lion's share and not only thanks to the poems of troubadours: love also dominates poetry of the Jews or Byzantines, the dress of young ladies, the elegy of a bird likened to a lover, dancing and the erotic function of games and wine (the latter presented in a more negative fashion).

Love should lead to marriage, but some girls prefer a convent life. Conjugal love between people of different social classes is frowned upon, but a wedding feast can be a princely affair, unsurpassed. Once married, don't forget to take your marriage certificate if you travel across frontiers. And we must not overlook the impediments to sexual life and good marriages: adultery, rape and prostitution. If all goes well and the marriage follows its allotted course, children are born – unfortunately into gross inequality. The sons of King Alfred each inherited £500, his daughters received only £100. And then, as they say, one dies; rarely in that distant epoch did one live to grow old and senile, a terrible situation both for the carers and those they look after.

In conclusion, one must render a final homage to this armful of wonderful texts, by noting that neither the mysteries of the year zero (the birth of Christ!), nor those of the Black Death of 1348, that great rupture of the medieval centuries, have escaped the shrewd eyes of our compiler. Judith Herrin knows how to focus on events, when necessary. But this is a way of saying that she defies categorisation, avoiding historical trends and fashions of all sorts, more American than British in fact. And we can forget the 'postmodern', which does not seem to be her cup of tea. Instead, we have a wonderful *Miscellany*, what our Belgian friends would call with their comic turn of invention, a *Mischpopott*; or as we would say, in the best and most tasteful sense, a *pot-pourri*.

EMMANUEL LE ROY LADURIE
Paris, October 1999

cenes from medieval life often appear familiar, intensely human and recognisable, yet also distant. They depict the everyday concerns of people who loved, worried, feasted, starved and prayed across a vast area from Scandinavia to Constantinople, from Ireland to Sicily, and from Spain to Jerusalem, for nearly a thousand years. Many recorded their fears, jokes and anxieties, especially with their health and pains, as well as their delights. In this miscellany I have tried wherever possible to select their own words from poems, chronicles, wills, romances, epitaphs, letters and legal regulations, all translated into modern English, rather than

opinions put into their mouths by others. Drawn from history but in no way a history, *A Medieval Miscellany* is a mosaic, necessarily incomplete, whose colourful stones have been gathered from every corner and period of the medieval world. I have pressed them into a rough seasonal pattern which is accompanied by the marvellous reproductions of medieval images selected by Linda and Michael Falter. We hope the combination will allow the reader to enjoy the presence and experience something of this way of life that is so remote from ours, despite many similarities.

The chronological range of this material, from the sixth to the fifteenth century, reflects a long, slow process of change, from the period still dominated by inherited patterns of Roman rule, to the humanistic world of the Renaissance city inhabited by Boccaccio and Petrarch. Despite this dramatic transformation, all the sources represent something distinctly medieval, a word that derives from the idea of the Middle Ages, *medium aevum*, a period between the ancient and the modern worlds.

Inevitably, the selection of texts from different points in such a long 'Middle Age' means there are some contradictions ⁄ for instance, the canon of 692 proscribing public entertainments throughout the week after Easter Sunday, and reports of fairs and fiestas later associated with Easter. Yet in both responses we can appreciate the centrality of the Church in the medieval world and the significance of its major feasts, which established the basic calendar for people who lived in the Middle Ages. Even if people had difficulty calculating the date (see 'The Calendar', page 33), their year was marked as much by the cycle of Christian festivals as by the changing seasons.

The medievals were aware of the existence of non-Christians, Jews, pagans, even of those in the remote world of the Great Khan of China, as well as heretics excluded from the Church for wrong belief and practice. But the vast majority knew no alternative to the Christian creed. The underlying framework of Christian belief formed their daily lives and they lived by its dogmas to the best of their ability. This also means that they were critical of its clerics and enjoyed jokes at their

expense. Nor did the church authorities uproot a deep tradition of secular humour, which flourished in the form of tales told around the fire at night: epics of ancient combat, romances peopled with superhuman figures, tales set in fabulous foreign lands, fables of talking beasts and stories of proverbial wisdom, strength and vengeance. War, pilgrimage, exploration and trade took medieval people to distant places with non-Christian traditions, which produced their share of fascinating reports. These surface not only in the great epics and romances of the Middle Ages, but also in accounts by modest pilgrims and travellers.

It was Anthony Cheetham's idea to produce *A Medieval Miscellany* and I would like to thank him and his colleagues at Weidenfeld and Nicolson for persuading me to select the texts to accompany the exquisite manuscript illustrations. Preparing this book was a delight. Many individuals helped with suggestions, not all of which could be incorporated. I particularly thank the following for their assistance: Teofilo Ruíz, Katherine Holman, George Baloglou, Charlotte Roueché and Peter Ricketts for their previously unpublished translations of foreign works. Thanks also go to: John Gillingham, Janet Nelson, Michael Richter, Bibi Sawyer, Linda Falter, William North, Joan Burchardt, Georgina Capel, Tamara Barnett-Herrin and Anthony Barnett.

JUDITH HERRIN

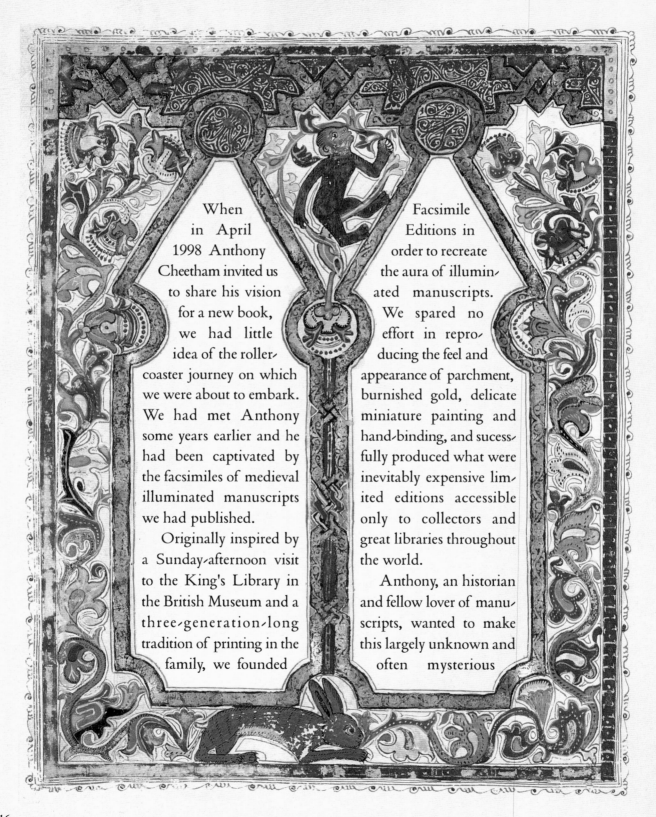

When in April 1998 Anthony Cheetham invited us to share his vision for a new book, we had little idea of the roller-coaster journey on which we were about to embark. We had met Anthony some years earlier and he had been captivated by the facsimiles of medieval illuminated manuscripts we had published.

Originally inspired by a Sunday-afternoon visit to the King's Library in the British Museum and a three-generation-long tradition of printing in the family, we founded Facsimile Editions in order to recreate the aura of illuminated manuscripts. We spared no effort in reproducing the feel and appearance of parchment, burnished gold, delicate miniature painting and hand-binding, and sucessfully produced what were inevitably expensive limited editions accessible only to collectors and great libraries throughout the world.

Anthony, an historian and fellow lover of manuscripts, wanted to make this largely unknown and often mysterious

world of manuscripts accessible to a wider public; and how better to achieve this than to combine medieval texts and art in order to depict for modern book-buyers the skill and inner life of medieval artists and scribes.

In over twenty years of work we have examined many of the world's greatest collections and have published facsimiles of some of their finest manuscripts. Our knowledge of these collections and our own substantial library of images enabled us to select beautiful manuscripts to illustrate the texts. We hope our captions will add to the appeal of the images and explain what they may have meant to their patrons.

There are many people we wish to thank for their help and inspiration, but our gratitude must go first to Anthony Cheetham for entrusting us with his vision, to Michael Dover for helping us execute it and to Judith Herrin for her fascinating text selections. We would also like to thank David Bussey, Amos Davis, Michel Garel, Raphael Loewe, Mauricio Hatchwell Toledano, Judith McLaren, Michael Pächt, Chris Rawlings, Brian Rich, Ruth Rosenthal, Michael Salem, Jeremy Schonfield and Nice Ugolotti Serventi for their help and support.

Bernadette Byrne at Clinton Smith worked all hours to help complete this book; and we could not have achieved the precision of detail without the dedicated teamwork of our colleagues at Graphicolor and Grafiche Milani in Italy.

None of this, needless to say, would have been possible without the scribes and illuminators themselves, many of them anonymous, whose work has been 'borrowed' for this book. We can only hope they would have approved of the way we have ensured that they will now be able to speak to a wider public.

And lastly, we must thank our wonderful sons, Gideon and Joseph, who in the midst of examinations have put up gracefully with the turmoil and excitement of this Medieval Miscellany.

LINDA AND MICHAEL FALTER

Spring

A late thirteenth-century spring song by the poet Nahum, a Jew from Spain.

Winter is gone, gone is my sorrow. The fruit-tree is in flower, and my heart flowers with joy.

The spikenards, as one, give forth their scent; the orchard of rare fruits is in full blossom. The hearts of friends are filled with merriment. O hunted gazelle who escaped far from my hut, come back, come drink my mulled wine and my milk!

Sorrows fled the day the flower-beds revived, fenced in by myrtles, braided with embroideries. Swiftly, then, all cares took flight. I am surrounded by coffers full of perfumes, dripping liquid myrrh. The boughs of the nut-tree trail low along my couch.

Trees of delight sway among the shadows: assia on the left, aloes on the right. With an emerald-coloured cup, ringed [with gold], and garnet-coloured wine, mixed with dew, I shall forget the misery and grief hidden deep in my heart.

What made my beloved, who used to graze between my fawn [-like breasts], leave me and take to the woods? Come to the arms of your dearest, who sings of her longing for you. O, my fair love, light the western lamp for me. In you, towering cherub, my flame will burn anew.

1 Top: The opening page of the Book of Job. In the Talmud, it states that 'God gave to Job a foretaste of the bliss of paradise'.

Love

This definition of love occurs in the
Romance of Akrites, *a Byzantine epic probably
written down in the eleventh century.*

Love produces kissing and kissing desire;
desire causes cares, worries and reflection
and threats and danger and separation from parents;
it fights against the sea, it recks nothing of fire;
and one in a state of desire loses his reason for love ⁄
he thinks nothing at all of cliffs and rivers;
he thinks vigils are rest and passes plains.
And all of you who are tormented for the love of a maid
have heard in writing of those famous Hellenes;
of how many torments they too endured for the sake of desire.
Consider, readers, those heroes
the Hellenes, those wonderful and famous soldiers,
and all that came to pass for the sake of that Helen,
when they defeated all Asia
and were all made glorious by their exceeding valour ⁄
and yet in their case too, when it came to matters of
love none could resist.

I Opposite: Troilus and Criseyde from a
French prose translation of Boccaccio's
Filostrato, written and illuminated *c.* 1480.

The Greek Anthology *contains a collection of amorous epigrams by Meleager put together in the sixth century. These two are devoted to Zenophilia.*

Already the white violet is in flower and narcissus that loves the rain, and the lilies that haunt the hillside, and already she is in bloom, Zenophilia, lover's darling, the sweet rose of Persuasion, flower of the flowers of spring. Why laugh ye joyously, ye meadows, vainglorious for your bright tresses? More to be preferred than all sweet-smelling posies is she.

The noise of Love is ever in my ears, and my eyes in silence bring their tribute of sweet tears to Desire. Nor night nor daylight lays love to rest, and

already the spell has set its well-known stamp on my heart. O winged Loves, is it that you are able to fly to us, but have no strength at all to fly away?

21

Mutual Love

This comes from an early twelfth-century correspondence between a man and woman, both unnamed, in the region of Troyes, northern France.

The more I drink my fill of your sweetness, the more I thirst. All my wealth has gathered in you alone, all I have power to do has its source in you. So, that we may devote ourselves to each other, you are I and I am you.

Love's Radiance

A Hebrew poem, 'The Laundress', by Judah Halevi (1075–1141).

My love washes her clothes in the water of my tears and spreads them out in the sun of her beauty. She has no need of spring-water, she has my two eyes; nor of the sun, she has her own radiance.

1 Tacuinum of Paris ⁄ *Coitus*: Is the union of two in order to introduce the sperm. *Optimum*: That which lasts until all the sperm has been emitted. *Uses*: It preserves the species. *Dangers*: Harmful to those who have cold and dry breathing. *Neutralization of the Dangers*: With sperm producing foods.

Fortune-telling

Predicting the future was a common activity, but one regularly condemned by the Church. In this regulation the Eastern bishops, gathered in council in 692, provide details of the many varied forms of ancient prophesy and condemn them all.

Those who have recourse to diviners, or to so-called 'centurians', or to any such persons, in order to learn from them whatever it is they want to discover, shall be subject to the canonical penalty of six years, in accordance with the decrees made by the Fathers not long ago in such matters. The same penalty ought to be inflicted on those who keep bears in tow and other such animals in order to deceive and cause mischief to the more simple-minded, haranguing the throng with fortune and fate and genealogy and other such words used in the trumpery of imposture, as well as the so-called cloud-chasers, sorcerers, purveyors of amulets and diviners.

I A fortune-telling tract from the thirteenth century made at the Abbey of St Albans by the monk Matthew Paris. Socrates, with Plato at his shoulder is writing predictions. During the Middle Ages, both philosophers were regarded as diviners.

II The idols made by the immigrants to Israel. A fiery idol extends its hand towards a naked boy while Nibhaz, a dog idol, protects Tartak shown as a naked couple (entwined, a symbol of fornication).

Whitsun

The Romance of Horn describes the celebration of Whitsun in late twelfth-century Norman England. The young hero, Horn, is chosen as cup bearer to the king.

They assembled at Pentecost for the great annual feast which was handsomely celebrated. Many mighty lords came from many regions, and their wives with them. Magnificent ladies, thus conferring more honour on the king's great court. Herland the seneschal was in charge of the court... Horn accompanied him, his face admired by all: no lady seeing him was not deeply affected and troubled by the pains of love. His well-cut tunic was of fine cloth, his hose close-fitting, his legs straight and slender. A short mantle hung from his shoulders, its strings untied to allow him to do whatever he was ordered...

Horn served the king well with the cup that day. He carefully scanned the rows and made many a round for he wanted no one discontented with his service. Thus he willingly had them all well served. Lord! How they praised his bearing and complexion now! No lady seeing him did not love him and want to hold him softly to her under an ermine coverlet, unknown to her lord, for he was the paragon of the whole court.

Love Condemned

In his compendium of advice, Matfre Ermengaud, the late thirteenth-century Provençal poet denounces certain aspects of love.

And they want to joust all day, be in tournaments, dance with ladies; and know for sure that the Devil leads their dance, and Satan so enflames their folly and so fires their passion that, through an excess of love, he makes them worship their ladies; for, since they should love the Creator with true love, with all their heart, their soul and all their understanding, so they love their ladies sinfully, and because of this they make him their deity. And know that, in worshipping them, they are in truth worshipping Satan and make their god the treacherous devil, Satan, Belial.

Love of Christ

Margery Kempe, an English visionary and mystic (c. 1373–c. 1440), caused great disturbance throughout Christendom because of her intense feelings of love for Christ and the Virgin. She went on pilgrimages to Compostela and Jerusalem, as the following passage indicates.

When she [Margery] knew that she was going to cry, she held it in as long as she could, and did all that she could to withstand it or else to suppress it, until she turned the colour of lead... And when the body might no longer endure the spiritual effort, but was overcome with the unspeakable love that worked so fervently in her soul, then she fell down and cried astonishingly loud...

And thus she did on the Mount of Calvary: she had as true contemplation in the sight of her soul as if Christ had hung before her bodily eye in his manhood. And when through dispensation of the

high mercy of our sovereign saviour, Christ Jesus, it was granted to her to behold so truly his precious tender body, all rent and torn with scourges, more full of wounds than a dove-cote ever was of holes, hanging upon the cross with the crown of thorns upon his head, his blessed hands, his tender feet nailed to the hard wood, the rivers of blood flowing out plenteously from every limb, the grisly and grievous wound in his precious side shedding out blood and water for her love and her salvation, then she fell down and cried with a loud voice, twisting and turning her body amazingly on every side, spreading her arms out wide as if she would have died, and could not keep herself from crying and these physical movements, because of the fire of love that burned so fervently in her soul with pure pity and compassion.

Love of God

Catherine of Siena wrote to Cardinal Iacopo Orsini in 1374.

Dearest and very loved father in Christ Jesus, I Caterina, servant and slave of the servants of Jesus Christ, am writing to you in his precious blood. I long to see you by the same blazing

divine clarity that moved God to draw us from within himself, from his infinite wisdom, so that we might share in and enjoy his supreme eternal good...

For God was so engrafted into humanity that one who was both God and human ran like one in love to the shameful death of the cross. This incarnate Word wanted to be engrafted onto that tree. And it was not the cross or the nails that held him there; these were not strong enough to hold the God-Man. No, it was love that held him there...

Love is so powerful that it makes one heart and one will of lover and beloved. Whatever the one loves, so does the other; if it were otherwise, it would not be perfect love. I have often noticed that when we love something - either because it would be useful to us or because it would give us some gratification or pleasure - we don't care what sort of abuse or injury or pain we might have to endure to get it; the effort means nothing to us; we are concerned only with satisfying our desire for the thing we love.

Oh dearest father, let us not disgrace ourselves before the children of darkness! What a shame that would be for the children of light - I mean God's servants chosen and taken from the world, and especially those who have been set as flowers and pillars in the garden of holy Church! You ought to be a fragrant flower, not a stinking weed. You should be clothed in purity's white, fragrant with patience and blazing with love, magnanimous and generous, not stingy...

There is only one thing to do then, and that is to invest our affection, our desire, our love in something stronger than ourselves – I mean in God, the source of all strength. He is our God who loved us without being loved. And once we have discovered and experienced such a gentle love, strong beyond all other strength, we cannot cling to or desire any other love but him. Apart from him there is nothing at all we seek or want...

I San Raphaele in an Italian Book of Hours   II Santa Catherina. Italian Book of Hours, fifteenth century.

I Above: Astrologer with an astrolabe.

II Below: Ezekiel's vision of four creatures holding the seven planetary spheres.

Astrology

Anna Komnene (1083–1153/4) wrote a history of her father, the Byzantine Emperor Alexios I Komnenos, in which she displays her wide learning and intellectual interests.

...the following are the facts about astrological prophecies. The discovery is fairly recent, and the science of it was not known to the ancients. For this method of divination did not exist in the time of Eudoxus, the greatest of all astronomers, neither did Plato have any knowledge of it... Now these [astrologers] observe the hour of the birth of the persons about whom they intend to prophesy, and fix the cardinal points and carefully note the disposition of all the stars, in short they do everything that the inventor of this science bequeathed to posterity and which those who trouble about such trifles understand. We, also, at one time dabbled a little in this science, not in order to cast horoscopes

(God forbid!), but by gaining a more accurate idea of this vain study to be able to pass judgment upon its devotees.

There was no dearth of astrologers at that time... a famous Egyptian, Alexandreus, was consulted by many and used to give most accurate forecasts in many cases, not even using the astrolabe, but [he] made his prophecies by a certain casting of the dice. There was nothing magical about that either... When the Emperor [Alexios I] saw how the young people flocked to him and regarded

the man as a species of prophet, he himself consulted him twice and each time Alexandreus gave very correct answers. But the Emperor was afraid that harm might come to many from it and that all would be led away to the vain pursuit of astrology, so he banished him from the capital...

Later again, a man called Catanances from Athens came to the capital... and when questioned by some about the date of the Emperor's death, he foretold it as he thought, but was proved wrong in his prognostication. It happened, however, that the lion which was kept in the palace died that day, after four days' fever, so the vulgar considered that the prophecy of Catanances had been accomplished.

Misfortune

The Spanish poet, Abraham Ibn Ezra (1092–1169), wrote this short poem on misfortune in Hebrew.

Out of Luck
However I struggle, I cannot succeed, for my stars have ruined me:
If I were a dealer in shrouds, no one would die as long as I lived.

I Above: Vexed at being ignored by their Prince, a group of astrologers in a certain kingdom decided to rouse the people to overthrow him. Hearing of this, the King's concubine warned the King, forestalling the plot. The astrologers, however, were unaware of the developments and are seen here reading signs for an auspicious date on which to launch the insurrection against the Prince.

II Right: Balaam, according to legend, was one of three seers who prophesied that Moses would destroy Egypt.

Fortune

In The Book of Chivalry, *Geoffroi de Charny, a French knight who died on the battlefield of Poitiers in 1356, warns against fickle fortune.*

Do not put too much faith in people who have risen above others by good fortune, not merit, for this will not last: they can fall as quickly as they rise...

One should not put trust in the benefits of fortune which are not earned for fortune is fickle and is destined to come to an end... But those who are reputed to be wise and are not, and those who are reputed to have won honour through deeds of arms and are unworthy of this renown, and those who have been raised up to noble rank and great wealth and high estate, when people of that kind are elevated to such a good fortune... the foundation on which their height of fortune is based is so weak that it must crumble and collapse... They therefore suffer more from the descent through having mounted so high. Hence the proverb of the ancients is true: 'He that climbs higher than he should, falls lower than he would.'

I Joseph is led away in chains at the hands of the Moors.

II Top: The butler's and baker's dreams: 'How the master butler humbly gave the cup to the king, while the baker was hanged on the gallows and the birds ate his flesh.'

III Above: Joseph's dream: the eleven sheaves of his brothers' corn bow down before Joseph's, prophesying his supremacy over them.

IV Opposite top: Elementary education. The teacher sits with a whip at the ready, while an hourglass marks the time. The child writes down part of *The Golden Rule,* a text by Hillel the Older intended to show the profound importance of education in Jewish life. German, fourteenth century.

V Opposite: Five teachers and their students, Barcelona *c.* 1340.

A Teacher's Warning

A collection of letters, written by an unidentified scholar based in Constantinople in the tenth century, reveal typical problems with students. The Metropolitan is probably the patron of some young clerics who are failing to study seriously.

Letter 69: to Alexander, Metropolitan of Nicaea... I hesitated whether to write to you or not, but decided that I ought to. Children naturally prefer play to study: fathers naturally train them to follow good courses, using persuasion or force. Your children, like their companions, neglected their work and were in need of correction. I resolved to punish them, and to inform their father. They returned to work and studied diligently for some time. But they are now occupied with birds once again, and neglecting their studies. Their father, passing through the city, commented acidly on their conduct. Instead of coming to me, or to their uncles, they have run away to you or to Olympus. If they are with you, treat them mercifully as suppliants. Even if they have gone elsewhere, help them to return to the fold. You will have my gratitude.

Children

During the entrance of King Henry IV of Castile to the city of Jaén in 1464, the children were allowed a major role.

Close to half a league from the city, all the canons of the cathedral, the municipal officials came to meet the king... Five hundred knights very well dressed and some dressed in the Moorish fashion, with false beards and heavy wooden lances (*cannas*) came [to meet the king] and engaged in mock battle. Further along the road, thirty other men came dressed as Moorish women playing tambourines and bells and giving great cries [in the Moorish fashion]... And further along the road four thousand children came out of the city riding on wicker horses and playing music, plus another one thousand children armed with wicker crossbows and also engaged in mock battle.

The Miracle of the Blind Boy

The miraculous cure of a small boy, abandoned by his parents, is recorded in the Book of Miracles of Sainte Foy, compiled in the eleventh century.

[The fugitive parents] left behind at home a son almost five years old... When the dead man's kindred saw the little boy and understood that his father... had fled... they were impelled by the same Furies who drove Orestes to slay his mother! They seized the little boy and, disdaining to kill such an insignificant person, they pierced the pupils of his eyes with sharp, pointed sticks and left him half dead.

But omnipotent God, to Whom is left the care of the wretched, was present for this boy abandoned by his parents, and He did not deprive the boy of His usual mercy. For the men of that village lifted him from the ground and carried him down to the church door, and they instructed him that with the others who were sick or injured he should beg alms from the people coming to pray. For several months he sought contributions there. Then one day when the sun was hastening to the west the inhabitants of Conques led him by the hand up to the holy virgin's altar. They eagerly requested of the highly renowned virgin that she deign to provide her customary mercy by granting a miracle for him. But I'll not waste time in long digressions. Just as a tiny little spark of fire set to a dead coal will cause it to brighten slowly until it glows with red heat, light sent down from heaven began to burn through the boy's clouded vision little by little, clearing the eyes that had been extinguished for so long. He reached out to touch the forms of things opposite him as if by the dim light of a dark moon, then he began to cry out with boyish glee that he could see a little... For with scarcely any delay the light continued to increase and he saw everything so clearly that he both recognized by sight and named whatever was shown to him. Everyone was filled with indescribable joy by this; the air rang mightily with their exuberant shouts; with their voices rivalling one another they made the whole basilica reverberate with declarations of praise. What more is there to say?... The boy was reciting the Psalmist's words, 'My father and my mother have left me, but the Lord has taken me up,' as the brothers carried him to the blessed virgin's holiest place. They nourished him with monastic support for the rest of his life, until death claimed what was owed and his soul flew up to the heavenly kingdoms.

The Calendar

Only from the sixth century onward was the system of calculating the date of the birth of Christ developed, but as the following text shows it was difficult to establish the AD method accurately.

5,954 years have passed from the beginning of the world to the era 792 [the equivalent of AD 754], which has now begun, the tenth year of the emperor Constantine, the fourth of Abd Allah, the *Amir Almuminim*, the seventh of Yusuf in the land of Spain, and the one hundred and thirty-sixth of the Arabs. If you wish, you may subtract four of these years in accordance with certain historians who diligently affirm this, computing the fifty-sixth year of the reign of Octavian to have expired in the 5,210th year of the world, and asserting that Christ was born in the forty-second year of the emperor Octavian. So it is in the sixth chapter of the first book of the *Ecclesiastical History* of lord Bishop Eusebius of Caesarea, as well as the *Chronicle* of

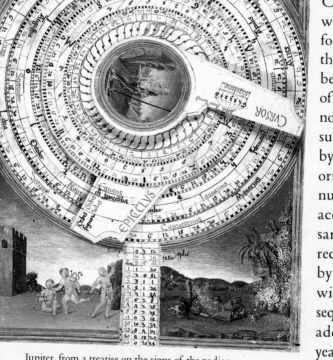

Jupiter, from a treatise on the signs of the zodiac

master Isidore and all the scriptures... When the fifth year of Julius Caesar was completed, 5,154 years of the world had passed. Adding the forty-two of Octavian, 5,196 years had passed from Adam to the nativity of Christ, which, as we said above, is four years less than 5,200... But because the years of the world have not been calculated sufficiently clearly by our predecessors so as to be numbered equally according to the same system or reckoned alike by all historians within a single sequence... we have added those four years in accordance with the many who contend that Christ was born in the year 5,200, lest we stray too far from the path about which so many distinguished men agree.

The White Cat

'The Student and his White Cat'
*was a poem written in the
margin of a manuscript of*
St Paul's Epistles *by an Irish student in
a monastery of Carinthia, in Austria,
probably in the ninth century. 'Bán' means
white.*

I Above: Rats were a constant scourge in the
Middle Ages. A certain preacher in Italy
would not take up his position until he was
assured that he would be provided
with a cat to stop vermin eating
his food and books.

II Opposite top: In around 1460,
it was customary for Jewish infants to
be swaddled in a shawl that restricted
movement.

III Opposite: The naked
figure is probably
Nebuchadnezzar, who is shown
riding a lion while forcing his jaws apart.

I and Pangur Bán, my cat
'Tis a like task we are at;
Hunting mice is his delight,
Hunting words I sit all night.

Better far than praise of men
'Tis to sit with book and pen;
Pangur bears me no ill-will,
He, too, plies his simple skill.

'Tis a merry thing to see
At our tasks how glad are we,
When at home we sit and find
Entertainment to our mind.

Oftentimes a mouse will stray
In the path of Pangur's way;
Oftentimes my keen thought set
Takes a meaning in its net.

'Gainst the wall
he sets his eye
Full and fierce and sharp and sly;
'Gainst the wall of knowledge I
All my little wisdom try.

When a mouse darts from its den,
O! how glad is Pangur then;
O! what gladness do I prove
When I solve the doubts I love.

So in peace our task we ply,
Pangur Bán, my cat, and I;
In our arts we find our bliss,
I have mine and he has his.

Practice every day has made
Pangur perfect in his trade;
I get wisdom day and night,
Turning darkness into light.

An Arranged Marriage

In the mid-tenth century, Bishop Paul of Monembasia in southern Greece collected stories, which he qualified as 'spiritually beneficial'. This one was recorded by a monk returning from Rome, who discovered a naked woman on an Aegean island. She told him her life history.

I am of the Helladôn country most worthy father, from the city of Larissa, the daughter of poor parents. When they died and left me an orphan, one of the ruling class took pity on me and received me into his house. He nourished me and raised me with care as though I were his own daughter. When I came of age that Christ-loving man married me to his only son as his wife, paying no attention to my poverty and lowly birth. When this was done, my husband's kin-folk and friends reviled him daily, saying: 'What is this your father has done to you; a woman of your own social standing was never found for you; and he has given you this penniless and low-born wife?' The son would answer: 'I am pleased with whatever my holy father has done for me. Since he raised her and knew her to be [a woman] of great value and beauty, his first considerations were not riches and noble birth, but virtue which is attractive to God; and that is what he gave me.' But even though my husband answered his kinsfolk like this, they did not stop reviling him. When I saw him one day after being reproached like this by his friends and relatives, I said to him: 'For the love of God, my husband, let me go into a monastery and you take a dis-tinguished and illustrious wife of your own rank.' He said: 'I set no account whatever on their foolish talk. I am pleased with what my holy father did for me.' Yet... they still went on making their foolish and contemptuous remarks to him.

Seeing him being persecuted by them like this, I decided to run away, and that is what I did. Unknown to anyone, I got up during the night and fled, all alone, taking nothing with me but the clothes I stood in. I came to the shore and I found a boat in which I embarked. With God's guidance I came to this island - without having realised that I was pregnant. I have strange and wonderful things to tell you, man of God: how from the time of my arrival here (suffering from fatigue and hunger) I gathered plants as food for this miserable body. In that way I just managed to stay alive and to nourish the child in my womb. But who can narrate the mighty and remarkable wonders of God? When the nine months had passed by I gave birth to a male child. I cut up the clothes I was wearing to make swaddling clothes for him and I raised him, by the unspeakable mercies of God who makes and directs all things according to his will and desire. [The child] is now just thirty years old and naked, as am I. Every day, together with me, he offers hymns to God with his thoughts turned to heaven, himself a reflection of divine beauty. Every day I have implored God to... send a priest to illuminate my son by holy baptism. And behold, the Lord has not refused my prayer but has sent you, his servant, to fulfil my desire.

Advice to an Officer

In the eleventh century, a retired Byzantine general, Kekaumenos, addressed a collection of moral stories and anecdotes full of advice to his sons.

When you are at leisure, and not busy with military duties, read military handbooks and histories, and the books of the church. Don't say: 'What benefit is there for a soldier from dogmas and church books?'; for you will benefit a great deal. And, if you pay careful attention, you will gather from them not merely dogmas, and edifying stories, but also maxims of intelligence, of morality and of strategy; for nearly all the Old Testament is stories of strategy.

A diligent reader will also gather maxims of intelligence, as well as many from the New Testament. I want you to be such a man that everyone may marvel at your courage, and your good planning, and your knowledge and eloquence; and if you adopt and observe these rules you will be happy. I drew these things up for you ⁄ which are not in any other military manual nor in any other book ⁄ I drew them up from my own reflections, and from real experience; for they will benefit you a great deal. Follow up the stratagems of the ancients as well; you won't find these things there; but you'll find other, better things, marvellous and full of wisdom.

I Above and above, right: Gospels. In the entombment scenes, the physical act of burial is turned into a lamentation for the dead Christ. Constantinople, 1050–1100.

Dress

In 692 the assembled bishops of Eastern Christendom met in council in Constantinople and regulated the style of dress appropriate for young girls and women taking monastic vows.

... Those who are to be promoted to the holy monastic habit are first dressed by those presenting them in silk and all manner of other raiment, as well as ornaments embellished with gold and jewels; and then, as they approach the altar, are divested of this rich attire and straightway are given the blessing to wear the monastic habit and are clothed in the black garment; we decree that henceforth this should not be done. For it is iniquitous that one who through her own choice has renounced every worldly joy and has espoused the life according to God... should again be reminded by this worthless and transitory adornment of those things which she has already consigned to oblivion... For if, as is natural, one little tear should escape, those who watched might not suppose that it came from her attitude toward the ascetic combat, but on account of quitting the world and worldly things.

1 Above: The richness of worldly dress that nuns renounce. 'A woman of valour who can find? For her price is far above rubies.' The Book of Proverbs, final chapter.

Eultate deo
adiutori nro:
iubilate deo
iacob.

Sumite
psalmum t

date tympanum: psaltium iocun
dum cum cythara.

Buccinate in neomenia tuba: in
insigni die sollempnitatis uestre.

Quia preceptum in israel est: et iu
dicium deo iacob.

Testimonium in ioseph posuit illud
cum exiret de terra egypti: linguam
quam n nouerat audiuit.

Diuertit ab oneribz dorsum eius: f

The Gift of a Book

Petrarch gives a much-loved copy of The Confessions of St Augustine *to a younger friend.*

To Father Luigi Marsili, from Arquà,
7 January 1374

... You ask me for a certain little book. I send it to you gladly as a gift. I should do so the more gladly if it were in the same condition as it was when given me by that Dionysius of your order, eminent student of sacred literature, a man of distinction in all things, and a most kind father to me. But as in my restless youth I was a wanderer by nature, I carried the book through most of Italy and through France and Germany because I was delighted with its substance, with its author, and with its easy portable size. Thus by constant use hand and book became so inseparable that they seemed to grow together. I omit various tumbles on land and in rivers; but once at Nice we were plunged into the sea together. We should certainly have perished, had not Christ rescued us both from imminent peril. Thus travelling with me it has grown old with me, and in its decrepitude it cannot be read by an old man without great difficulty. Now, long after leaving its Augustinian quarters, it returns home again; and again, I suspect, it will make its journeys with you. Accept it then as it is and enjoy it.

Farewell, be happy, and pray to Christ for me whenever you approach his table.

I An elderly Italian Jew studies books with velvet bindings, leather thongs and metal clasps.

II Opposite page: A magnificent historiated letter from an English fourteenth-century Psalter. The knight in the margin is holding the shield of the baronial family who commissioned the manuscript.

A New Fair

Medieval fairs were often held on holy days, when crowds would congregate at shrines, on the feasts of Easter, All Saints (1 November) or Epiphany (6 January). Matthew Paris describes how a new date was fixed on 13 October in 1248, to mark the feast of St Edward.

And the lord king ordered it to be officially announced and proclaimed throughout the whole city of London and elsewhere by public crier that he had instituted a new fair to be held at Westminster to continue for a full fortnight, and, in order that the Westminster fair should more copiously abound with people and merchandise, he absolutely forbade on penalty of weighty forfeiture and fine all markets usually held in England for such a period of time, for instance the fairs at Ely and elsewhere, as well as all trade normally carried on in London both in and out of doors. As a result, a vast crowd of people flocked there as if to the most famous fair, and so the translation of the blessed Edward and the blood of Christ was amazingly venerated by the people assembled there. But all those who exhibited their goods for sale there suffered great inconvenience because of the lack of roofs apart from canvas awnings; for the variable gusts of wind, usual at that time of year, battered the merchants so that they were cold, wet, hungry and thirsty. Their feet were dirtied by the mud and their merchandise spoilt by rain. When they sat down there at table, those who normally took their meals at home by the

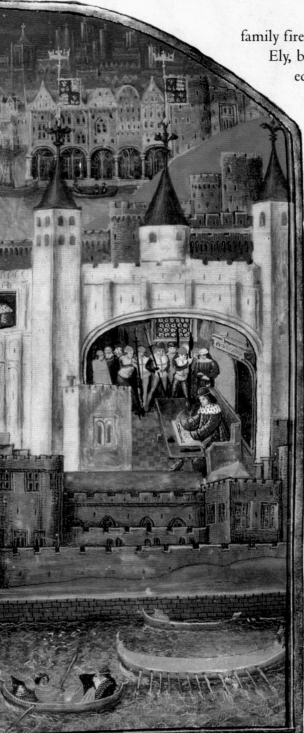

family fireside could not stand this discomfort. The bishop of Ely, because of the loss of his fair at Ely, which the royal edict had suspended, made a very serious complaint about this to the king for introducing such novelties to the detriment of his subjects. But he gained nothing except empty words and comforting promises of future consolation.

Rag Day

Students have contributed their own songs to the secular repertoire. This anonymous one is preserved in a twelfth-century collection.

Hooray! Today's a holiday:
a happy day ⁄ a jolly day:
a day to strum guitars and play
the good old songs the good old way:
to love your neighbour and display
the side of you that's bright and gay:
and students most of all, for they
excel at parties anyway!

So throw your books and slates away ⁄
there's food for which you needn't pay
forget the works of Ovid, eh? ⁄
and tell his friends to go and play.
Never mind what people say
youth needs its recreations:
since the world is making hay
let's join the celebrations!

↑ Left: A miniature of the Tower of London, with London Bridge and the City in the background. Manuscript of the poems of Charles d'Orleans, *c.* 1480–3.

Dress Sense

Writing in the fourteenth century, Geoffroi de Charny describes the dangers of fine clothing and counsels humility among those seeking to dress fashionably.

If anyone is thus elegantly dressed and in good fashion, as befits a young man, it should not be done through pride nor should Our Lord be forgotten; but be careful not to spruce yourself up so much that you do not remember God, for, if you do not remember God, God will not remember you. But one should dress well when in company with other young people and to fit in with them; and it is a fine and good thing to spend one's youth in honest fashion, and those who spend it thus should praise God all their lives.

As for the youth of noble ladies, damsels and other women of high rank, it can indeed be said that... it is fitting to wear fine circlets, coronetals, pearls, precious stones, rings, embroidery, to be beautifully dressed, their heads and bodies well adorned according to what is right and fitting for each person to do; it is much more suitable for them to wear fine adornments than for men, for young damsels sometimes achieve better marriages when they are seen in rich apparel which suits them.

These rich ornaments should be left to them [noble ladies and damsels]. For those who have the will to rise to great achievement, how can they better adorn themselves than by being equipped for it by all the good qualities? They can do so by being men of worth, wise, loyal, without arrogance, joyful, generous, courteous, expert, bold and active...

1 Opposite: Dancing in the Garden of Love . Guillaume de Loris and Jean de Meun from *Le Roman de la Rose*, Flanders, 1490–1500.

A Scarlet Dress

One of the Canterbury Pilgrims, the Wife of Bath, described her life and her five husbands in the Prologue *to her tale, c. 1386.*

My fifth and last ⁄ God keep his soul in health!
The one I took for love and not for wealth,
Had been at Oxford not so long before
But had left school and gone to lodge next door,
Yes, it was to my godmother's he'd gone
God bless her soul! Her name was Alison.
She knew my heart and more of what I thought
Than did the parish priest, and so she ought!
She was my confidante, I told her all.
For had my husband pissed against a wall

Above: Revellers in an orchard. Lutenists and Singers by the Masters
of the Prayer Books. From *Le Roman de la Rose*, Flanders 1490⁄1500.

Or done some crime that would have cost his life,
To her and to another worthy wife
And to my niece, because I loved her well,
I'd have told everything there was to tell.
And so I often did, and Heaven knows
It used to set him blushing like a rose
For shame, and he would blame his lack of sense
In telling me secrets of such consequence.

And so one time it happened that in Lent,
As I so often did, I rose and went
To see her, ever wanting to be gay
And go a-strolling, March, April and May,
From house to house for chat and village malice.

Johnny (the boy from Oxford) and Dame Alice
And I myself, into the fields we went.
My husband was in London all that Lent;
All the more fun for me ⁄ I only mean
The fun of seeing people and being seen

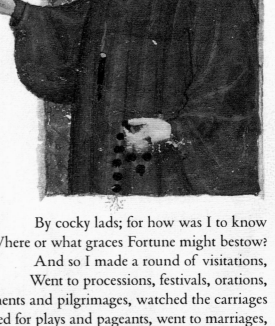

By cocky lads; for how was I to know
Where or what graces Fortune might bestow?
And so I made a round of visitations,
Went to processions, festivals, orations,
Preachments and pilgrimages, watched the carriages
They used for plays and pageants, went to marriages,
And always wore my gayest scarlet dress.

These worms, these moths, these mites, I must confess
Got little chance to eat it, by the way,
Why not? Because I wore it every day.

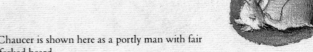

I Above: Chaucer is shown here as a portly man with fair
hair and a forked beard.

II Left: Opening page of Chaucer's *The Canterbury Tales*.

45

A Wedding Feast

The reception of the Infanta Doña Blanca on arrival in Castile to marry the Infante Don Enrique, in 1440.

The princess Doña Blanca, her mother the Queen, her brother the prince Don Carlos... and a retinue of ecclesiastical dignitaries and knights from the kingdoms of Aragon and Navarre also arrived... [They] continued on the way to Briviesca, where festivities were prepared for them and where all [the inhabitants] of the town welcomed them with much solemnity. Each of the guilds came out with their banners and theatrical skits, in the best possible fashion; and with great dances, great enjoyment and happiness. Following them came the Jews with the Torah and the Moors with the Koran [dancing] in the manner usually reserved for [the entry of] kings who come to rule a foreign country. There were also many trumpets, tambourines, drums and flute players which made such a great noise that it seemed as if a very large host was coming. On arriving in the town all together, they accompanied the Queen and the princess to the Count's palace. There the important people dismounted and repaired to a place where a collation was prepared, supplied with such a diversity of poultry, meats, fish, delicacies and fruits that it was a marvellous thing to see; the table and servers were set in a fashion becoming such great ladies. And they were served by knights and gentlemen and by richly dressed pages from the Count's household.

A tent was set, covered with an elegant tapestry and there were there also tables and servers for Don Alonso, bishop of Burgos, the prelates and foreign clergymen... The others were also fed abundantly in other tents. The feast lasted four days... In a chamber on the fourth floor [of the count's palace] there was a silver fountain pouring out wine, and people took as much of it as they wanted.

I Belshazzar's Feast. The divine curse is revealed to Belshazzar.

Warships

In the late ninth century, southern England suffered repeated attacks by the Danes established in East Anglia, which the Anglo-Saxon king countered by constructing special new ships.

Then King Alfred ordered 'long-ships' to be built with which to oppose the Viking warships. They were almost twice as long as the others. Some had sixty oars, some more. They were both swifter and more stable, and also higher, than the others. They were built neither on the Frisian nor on the Danish pattern, but as it seemed to Alfred himself that they would be most useful.

Then on a certain occasion in the same year six Viking ships came to the Isle of Wight and did considerable damage there, both in Devon and all along the sea-coast. Then the king ordered his men to set out with nine of the new ships, and they blocked them off in the estuary from the seaward end. Then the Vikings went out with three ships against them; and three were beached further up the estuary on dry land: the men had gone off inland. Then the English captured two of the three ships at the mouth of the estuary and killed the men. The other one escaped: the men on that one were also killed, except five, these got away because the English ships ran aground on that side of the channel where the Danish ships were beached, and all the others on the other side so that none of them could get to the others. But when the water had ebbed many furlongs from the ships, the Danes from the three beached ships then went to the other three English ships which were stranded on their side, and there they then fought... and of all the Frisians and English, sixty-two were killed, and of the Danes, 120. Then, however, the flood-tide came first to the Danish ships before the Christians could push theirs off, and so they rowed out and away. They were wounded by then to such an extent that they were unable to row past Sussex, but there the sea cast two of the ships on to the land, and then they were taken to Winchester to the king, and he ordered them to be hanged there. And the men who were in the one remaining ship made it back to East Anglia, severely wounded.

47

Warfare

In 1453 Sultan Mehmed brought up his cannon to end the siege of Constantinople. Emperor Constantine XI rallied the defenders against the Ottomans. On 29 May the final assault began.

The hour was already advanced, the day was declining and near evening and the sun was at the Ottomans' backs but shining in the faces of their enemies. This was just as the Sultan had wished; accordingly he

 gave the order first for the trumpets to sound the battle-signal, and the other instruments, the pipes and flutes and cymbals too, as loud as they could... a great and fearsome sound. Everything shook and quivered at the noise. After that the standards were displayed.

To begin, the archers and slingers and those in charge of cannon and the muskets, in accord with the commands given them, advanced against the wall slowly and gradually. When they got within bowshot, they halted to fight. And first they exchanged fire with the heavier weapons, with arrows from the archers, stones from the slingers, and then leaden balls from the cannon and muskets. Then, they closed with battleaxes and javelins and spears, hurling them at each other and being hurled at pitilessly in rage and fierce anger... This kept up till sunset...

Sultan Mehmed saw that the attacking divisions were very much worn out by the battle and had not made any progress worth mentioning... Immediately he brought up the divisions which he had been reserving for later on, men who were extremely well armed, daring and brave, and far in advance of the rest in experience and valour. They were the elite of the army: heavy infantry, bowmen, and lancers, and his own bodyguard, and along with them those of the division called Janissaries.

Calling on them and urging them to prove themselves now as heroes, he led the attack against the wall, himself at the head... With a loud and terrifying war-cry and with fierce impetuosity and wrath they advanced as if mad. Being young and strong and full of daring, and especially because they were fighting in the Sultan's presence, their valour exceeded every expectation. They attacked the palisade and fought bravely without any hesitation... and forced the defenders back inside...

The Emperor Constantine... took his stand in front of the palisade and fought bravely. Sultan Mehmed who happened to be fighting quite near by, saw that the palisade and the other part of the wall that had been destroyed were now empty of men and deserted by the defenders. Realising that the wall was deserted, he shouted out: 'Friends, we have the City, we have it!'... So saying he led them himself...

Now there was a great struggle and great slaughter among those stationed there. There the Emperor Constantine, with all who were with him, fell in gallant combat... After this the Sultan entered the City and looked about to see its great size, its situation, its grandeur and beauty, its teeming population, its loveliness, and the costliness of its churches and public buildings and of the private houses... When he saw what a large number had been killed, and the ruin of the buildings, and the wholesale ruin and destruction of the City, he was filled with compassion and repented not a little... Tears fell from his eyes as he groaned deeply and passionately: 'What a city we have given over to plunder and destruction!'

Opposite: The conquest of the city of Crator. From a manuscript by Jean de Bueil, Brittany.

Building

Abbot Suger of St Denis was very active in rebuilding the ancient abbey of St Denis in which the kings of France were buried. In the mid-twelfth century, he planned the extension to the main church described here.

Thus, when, with wise counsel and under the dictation of the Holy Ghost... that which we proposed to carry out had been designed with perspicuous order, we brought together an assembly of illustrious men, both bishops and abbots, and also requested the presence of our Lord, the Most Serene King of the Franks, Louis. On Sunday, the day before the Ides of July, we arranged a procession beautiful by its ornaments and notable by its personages. Carrying before ourselves, in the hands of the bishops and the abbots, the insignia of Our Lord's Passion, viz. the Nail and the Crown of the Lord, also the arm of the aged St Simeon and the tutelage of other holy relics, we descended with humble devotion to the excavations made ready for the foundations. Then, when the consolation of the Comforter, the Holy Spirit, had been invoked so that He might crown the good beginning of the house of God with a good end, the bishops... laid the first stones, singing a hymn to God and solemnly chanting the *Fundamenta ejus* to the end of the Psalm. The Most Serene King himself stepped down [into the excavations] and with his own hands laid his [stone]. Also we and many others, both abbots and monks, laid their stones. Certain persons also [deposited] gems out of love and reverence for Jesus Christ, chanting: *All thy walls are precious stones*. We, however,... anxious for what was still to be done and fearful of the changes of time, the diminution of persons and my own passing away, ordained in a common council of the brethren... an annual revenue for completing this work; namely one hundred and fifty pounds from the treasury... one hundred [derived from the offerings] at the fair, and fifty [from the offerings] at the feast of Saint Denis. In addition, fifty from the possession called Villaine... And we decreed that these two hundred pounds... be applied to the continuation of these works until, without any question, these edifices... will be entirely and honourably completed throughout, including their towers.

Travel Documents

A thirteenth-century note, probably inserted into a letter by the unknown author, reveals the difficulty of travelling from Ceuta in Morocco to Bijaya (Bougie) in Algeria with insufficient evidence of identification.

Furthermore, I inform you that I long and yearn for you, I also inform you that someone arrived here and told us that your son Nissim travelled from Ceuta to Bijaya, where the governor of the town found that a woman was in his company. He asked him: How is this woman related to you? He answered: She is my wife. However, when he was asked for her marriage certificate, he replied that she had none. Upon this the governor took all his goods and put him into prison. Nothing remained in his possession.

By God, do not tarry. Take note of this. Greetings. *And Peace.*

I Opposite: The Tower of Babel under construction in Mozarabic style. Spain, fifteenth century.

II Above: A procession of travellers drawn in Spain in 1340.

III Left: In this medieval ship, the artist fills in the hull with a brick like pattern, the crow's nest has spears in it and a red dragon forms the figurehead.

A Shepherd's Duty

An anonymous French text on estate management, dating from the thirteenth century, defines the duties and responsibilities of farm employees.

Each shepherd... ought to cover, enclose, and repair the folds, repair and do hedging, fences, and hurdles, and he and his watchdog ought to lie in the fold with the sheep.

He ought to pasture and feed his sheep well and watch over them well so that they are not killed

or tormented by dogs, stolen, lost, or exchanged and they do not pasture in forbidden moors, ditches, and bogs thereby contracting illness and rot through lack of supervision.

No shepherd ought to leave his sheep to go to fairs, markets and wrestling matches or to spend the evenings with friends or go to the tavern without asking for leave and putting a good keeper in his place to look after the sheep, so that no harm or loss occurs through his fault. All the sheep of the lord ought to be marked with the same mark, and no ewe

ought to be milked after the feast of the Nativity of Our Lady (8 September) because they are then slow to mate in the following year and the lambs will be worth less.

I This page: 'Image of the shepherd burning incense and sacrificing on the wood which is upon the altar'. Ibn Sahula, Fables of the Ancients, part of the Rothschild Miscellany, Italy 1479.

II Opposite page: The King of Navarre's bed catching fire. Froissart's, *Chroniques de France, c.*1480.

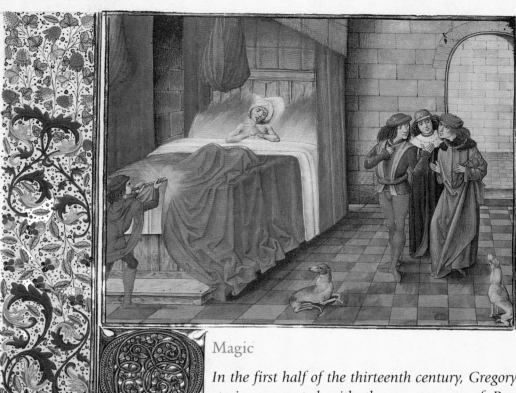

Magic

In the first half of the thirteenth century, Gregory collected stories connected with the monuments of Rome, many of which had ancient and unknown origins, hence their classification as Mirabilia *[Marvels].*

Here begins the account of the wonders of the city of Rome, which have been fashioned either by magic craft or by human labour... Among all the strange works which were once in Rome, the multitude of statues known as the 'Salvation of the Citizens' is to be much admired. By magic art statues were dedicated to all those peoples who were subject to Roman rule, and indeed there was no race or region under Roman authority which did not have its statue in this particular hall. A large portion of its walls still stand, and the vaults seem stark and inaccessible.

In this hall these statues stood in a row, each one having written on its breast the name of the race which it represented, and each wearing around its neck a bell made of silver, because silver is more resonant than other metals. And there were priests who watched over them, ever vigilant both by day and by night. If any nation dared to rise in rebellion against Roman rule, its statue would immediately move, causing the bell to ring, and at once a priest would write down its name and convey this to the government. Above this hall of statues there was a bronze soldier on horseback who would move in conjunction with the statue, aiming his lance at the race whose image had stirred. Warned in this unequivocal manner, without delay the Romans would dispatch an army to suppress that nation's rebellion, and they would often forestall their enemies before they could prepare their weapons and supplies, thus subjugating them easily and without bloodshed.

The Miracle of the Testicles

In the mid-seventh century, Stephen, a deacon of St Sophia, the Great Church of Constantinople, related how he was miraculously cured by St Artemios, whose shrine in the region of Oxeia was famous for the treatment of male genital disorders.

'In my testicles,' he said 'I suffered a rupture, whether from shouting acclamations or from a heavy weight, I can not really say. This happened to me a short time before Herakleios of blessed memory died (641) and out of shame I concealed myself for a considerable time, watching carefully for a chance to bathe alone in the small hours. At long last I disclosed the misfortune to my parents and after many treatments (how many!) had been performed on me, finally after taking counsel with them, I entrusted myself for surgery to the surgeons in the hospital of Sampson and I reclined in the hospital room near the entrance to the area devoted to eyes. After I had been treated all over for three nights and days with cold cauteries, surgery was performed on the fourth day. I will omit what horrible things I experienced while on my back.

To sum up everything, I state that I actually despaired of life itself at the hands of the physicians. After God, entreated by the tears of my parents, restored my life to me, and after the scar from the incision and the cautery had healed, and just as I was believing that I was healthy, a short time later the same condition recurred and so I reverted to my former state...

I had a plan to approach the holy martyr, as I had heard of his many great miracles. Still I was unwilling to wait in the venerable church, feeling ashamed before friends and acquaintances to be seen by them in such a condition. But I

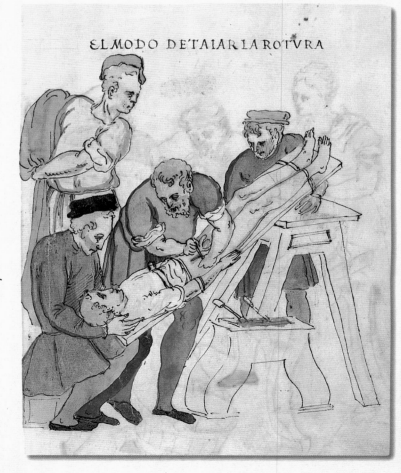

ELMODO DE TAIAR LA ROTVRA

1 Above: An operation for a scrotal hernia. Italy.

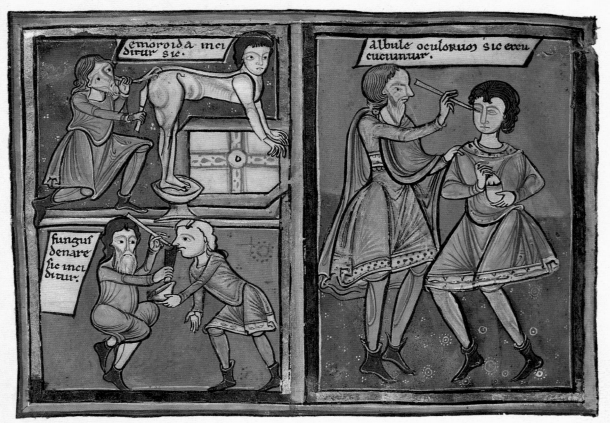

frequently used to pass by (for at that time, he said, I was staying in the Oxeia) and so I descended to the holy tomb of his precious relics and I cast some of his holy blessing *i.e. oil* on my testicles, hoping to procure a cure in this manner. And frequently I entreated him to deliver me from the troublesome condition...

After descending to the holy tomb, I found the doors in front open and I was astounded that they were open at such an hour. This was the doing of the martyr in his desire to pity me. Stretching out face down on the holy coffin, I straddled it and thus contrived to rub the corner of the same holy tomb on the spot where I was ailing. And with tears I spoke again to the martyr: "St Artemios, by God Who has given you the gift of cures, no doctor on earth will ever touch me again. So if you please, cure me. But if not, to your everlasting shame I will live thus without a cure." And after some days I went to the bath in the quarter of Anthemios, the one called Livanon, to bathe by myself at dawn in order not to be seen by anyone. And entering the hot chamber, I noticed that I still had the injury. But upon exiting, I had no injury, and recognizing the act of kindness on the part of God and the martyr which had befallen me... in thanksgiving... I do now glorify them proclaiming their deeds of greatness throughout my whole life.'

11 Top: The excision of haemorrhoids, removal of cataracts and the extirpation of nasal polyps. It was thought that cataracts were a whitish liquid that ran down from the brain. England, twelfth century.

Trading in India

Marco Polo recorded numerous details of the crops and products he noticed on his travels (1260–1295). Here he describes those from Gujarat in India.

There is pepper here in profusion and also ginger and indigo. There is also plenty of cotton, for the cotton trees grow here to a great height ⁄ as much as six paces after twenty years' growth. But when they reach this age they no longer produce cotton fit for spinning, but only for use in wadding or padded quilts. The growth of these trees is such that for up to twelve years they produce cotton for spinning, but from twelve to twenty an inferior fibre only.

Above: 'La cité de Polombe'. The black and white pepper harvest in India. France, *Livre des Merveilles c.* 1405.

The manufactures of this kingdom include great quantities of leather goods, that is, the tanned hides of goat and buffalo, wild ox and unicorn and many other beasts. Enough is manufactured to load several ships a year. They are exported to Arabia and many other countries... They also manufacture handsome mats of scarlet leather, embossed with birds and beasts and stitched with gold and silver of very fine workmanship... You must understand that these leather mats of which I speak are such as the Saracens sleep on, and very good they are for the purpose. They also make cushions stitched with gold, so splendid that they are worth fully six marks of silver... some are of such a quality that they are worth ten marks of silver.

II Above: 'Pygmies on the banks of the Ganges who find nourishment in the odours of the fruits.'

III Centre: The Book of Ezekiel, Alba Bible, Maqueda, Spain, 1422–30. The text describes how 'By the river upon the bank thereof... shall grow all trees for meat... and the leaf thereof for medicine'.

After Dinner Entertainment

During his first trip to Byzantium in 949, Liutprand, Bishop of Cremona, was greatly impressed by one after-dinner entertainment. His Latin text was sprinkled with Greek phrases, which are rendered in French in the following translation.

As for the various entertainments I saw there... one... was so remarkable that it will not be out of place to insert an account of it here. A man came in carrying on his head, without using his hands, a wooden pole twenty-four feet or more long, which a foot and a half from the top had a cross-piece three feet wide. Then two boys appeared, naked except for loin cloths round their middle, who went up the pole, did various tricks on it, and then came down head first, keeping the pole all the time as steady as though it were rooted in the earth. When one had come down, the other remained on the pole and performed by himself, which filled me with even greater astonishment and admiration. While they were both performing, their feats seemed barely possible; for, wonderful as it was, the evenness of their weights kept the pole up which they climbed balanced. But when one remained at the top and kept his balance so accurately that he could both do his tricks and come down again without mishap, I was so bewildered that the emperor himself noticed my astonishment. He therefore called an interpreter, and asked me which seemed the more wonderful, the boy who had moved so carefully that the pole remained firm, or the man who had so deftly balanced it on his head that neither the boys' weight nor their performance had disturbed it in the least. I said that I did not know which I thought *plus merveilleux* that is, more wonderful; and he burst into a loud laugh and said he was in the same case, he did not know either.

1 Humay at the Chinese Court. By Junayd *Khamsa* of Khvaju Kirman. Jalayirid style. Baghdad 1396.

פֶּן־דִּבֶּר תָּרֶר אֶלֵהֶם
אֲשֶׁר לֹא יְדַבֵּר עַל
הַמִּכְתָּב לַבַּיִת אֲשֶׁר שָׁמַר

On the Need for Discretion

In July 1347 Petrarch wrote to Cola di Rienzo from Avignon, where he was employed in the papal court of the Roman pontiffs, who were exiled there from 1313.

To Cola di Rienzo, Tribune of the Roman people

I do not know whether you are aware of, or suspect, or are entirely ignorant of, a certain fact. Do not suppose for a moment that the letters that you write from Rome remain long in the possession of those to whom they are addressed. On the contrary, everyone rushes to make a copy of them with as much earnestness, and circulates them around the pontiff's court with as much zeal, as if they were sent not by a man of our own race but by an inhabitant of another world or of the antipodes. All press round to interpret your epistles; and never was an oracle of the Delphic Apollo turned and twisted into so many different meanings. I therefore praise the caution that you have displayed up to now. Until now you have exerted great care in moderating your tone and have succeeded beyond reproach. I urge you and beg you to display greater and greater care in the future...

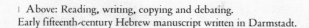

1 Above: Reading, writing, copying and debating.
Early fifteenth-century Hebrew manuscript written in Darmstadt.

I have witnessed several persons struck with amazement as they read, when they saw your self-assurance struggling with your modesty so as to leave only a doubtful victory; astonished when they saw that neither debasing fear nor swelling pride found admittance to that contest. I have seen others perplexed as to whether they should more deeply admire your deeds or your words...

Persevere, therefore, as you have begun. Always write as if everyone were to read, and not merely read, but as if they were about to set out from every shore and bear your message to every land. You have laid the strongest of foundations: truth, peace, justice, and liberty. Build on these. Whatever structure you erect will remain firm; and whoever hurls himself against it will be dashed to pieces. He who wars against truth will declare himself a liar; against peace, a restless spirit; against justice, a dishonest man; and if against liberty, an arrogant and shameless wretch.

War Personified

The Spanish poet, Samuel Hanagid (993–1056), observed:

War is at first like a beautiful girl with whom all men long to play, but in the end like a repulsive hag whose suitors all weep and ache.

1 'How the Tartars troubled the Sultan of Turkey and all his Court.' Mangu Khan, in his boat under attack before the walls of Hou-Tchou. From a fifteenth-century French travel book containing the description of Marco Polo's voyages entitled *Livre des Merveilles*.

I The destruction of Sodom. Talmudic sources attribute this to the angel Gabriel. In the dawn sky an angel is seen hurling fiery rocks onto the richly turreted city; flames are erupting from the windows and doors, human life has vanished and all is silence.

Summer Storms

An account by the anonymous chronicler attached to the monastery of Fulda, dated 870.

At Mainz the sky shone red like blood for many nights, and other portents were seen in the heavens. One night a cloud climbed up from the north and another from the south and east, and they exchanged bolts of lightning continuously. In the end they met overhead and as it were fought a great battle. All who saw this were amazed and afraid and prayed that these monstrous things might be turned to good. The lands around that same city were struck by two earthquakes. Several men gathering in the harvest in the district of Worms were found dead because of the heat of the sun, which was fiercer than usual. Many were also drowned in the Rhine.

II The destruction of Jericho. The Israelites, led by Joshua, encircle the town that tumbles down in the centre of the picture. Some blow trumpets, while others carry the Ark of the Covenant with the cherubim. Still others pray with their hands joined and the remaining men in armour advance, each with a spear in his right hand.

Ugly Feet

From the medieval Norse epic, The Saga of St Olav.

There was a man called Toraren Nevjolvson. He was an Icelander... not of great family, but he was wise and clever of speech, and bold in talk with princes. He was a great traveller and was abroad for long stretches of time. Toraren was an ugly man, and especially so because he was ill-shaped in the limbs. He had great ugly hands, but his feet were very much uglier...

King Olav had Toraren as a guest for some days and talked much with him. Toraren slept in the king's room. Early one morning the king lay awake, but the other men in the room were asleep; the sun had just risen, and there was much light within. The king saw that Toraren had stretched one foot forth from the bedclothes. He looked at the foot for a time; then they woke up in the room. The king said to Toraren: 'I have

ɪ The Lindisfarne Gospels. Miniature of St Matthew from the famous Latin manuscript of the four Gospels made about AD 698 in the Northumbrian island monastery of Lindisfarne. Eadfrith, its scribe and illuminator, later became Bishop of Lindisfarne.

been awake some time and I have seen a sight which seems of great worth; it is a man's foot, so ugly that I believe there will not be one uglier in the whole town,' and he bade the others look and see whether it seemed the same to them. And all who saw said truly that it was so. Toraren understood then what they were talking about and answered: 'There are few things so odd that you cannot expect to find the like to them, and it is most likely that it is so now.' The king said: 'I will not hold with it that you can find so ugly a foot, even if I should bet on it.' Then Toraren answered: 'I am ready to bet you that here in this house I can find an uglier foot.' The king said: 'Then shall the one of us who is right crave a boon of the other.' 'So shall it be,' said Toraren; he stuck forth from the bedclothes the other foot, and it was no whit fairer and the big toe was off too. Then said Toraren: 'Look here, O king, at another foot which is so much uglier as there is a toe off. I have won the bet.'

Summer Love

One of the famous twelfth-century lais *[tales] of Marie de France, 'The Nightingale' concerns two knights of Saint-Malo who lived in adjacent and strongly fortified houses.*

One had married a wife who was well-behaved, courteous and elegant... The other young man was a bachelor knight, unmarried, well-known among his peers for his bold exploits...

He fell in love with his neighbour's wife. He begged so hard and pleaded with her, and he was so excellent a man, that she came to love him more than anything in the world... They loved each other prudently and discreetly. They took care to conceal their behaviour and to guard against being perceived, disturbed, or suspected.

1 Pygmalion and Galatea. *Le Roman de la Rose.* France *c.* 1405.

They succeeded in this since they lived near each other... There was no barrier, nothing to separate them except a high wall of darkened stone. From the chambers where the lady slept she was able, when she stood at the window, to converse with her friend on the other side, and he with her. They were able to exchange their love tokens by tossing or throwing them. There was nothing to mar their happiness even though they could not come together to fulfil their desires...

For a long time they were in love, until summer came, when woods and fields grow green again and orchards bloom. Small birds sing sweetly from the flowering treetops. It's not surprising that whoever longs for love can think of this and nothing else...

At night when the moon shone and her husband lay sleeping, she would often steal from his side; with her cloak wrapped about her she would go to the window, for she knew her friend would be at his. This is how they lived, gazing at each other for most of the night. They derived pleasure from seeing each other, denied as they were a greater bliss. She stayed so often at the window and would get up out of bed so often at night, that her husband lost his temper, and more than once demanded to know the reason why she rose in this way and where she went. 'My husband,' replied the lady, 'anyone who hasn't heard the nightingale sing has not experienced joy in the world. That is why I go to stand at the window. I hear its sweet voice in the night... so intensely do I long to hear it, that I cannot close my eyes to sleep.'

When her husband heard what she said, he laughed with angry contempt. An idea occurred to him to trap the nightingale. He ordered the household servants to work on traps, nets and snares and to set them in the orchard. There wasn't a hazel or a chestnut tree anywhere that was not hung with nets or smeared with lime. Eventually they captured the nightingale. They took it alive to the lord, who was overjoyed when he saw it. He went to the lady's chambers. 'Madam, where are you? Come now, let us talk, I've used birdlime to catch this nightingale, the cause of your nightlong vigils. Now you'll be able to slumber in peace, as it will never bother you again.'

... In a fit of perversity he killed it. He villainously broke its neck with his two hands. He threw the dead bird at his wife so that the front of her gown was blood-ied over her breast. Then he went out of the room...

The lady took the little corpse and softly wept over it. She cursed those who had treacherously caught the nightingale... for they had killed a great joy... In a length of satin embroidered and inscribed in letters of gold thread she wrapped the body of the tiny bird. She called one of her servants and entrusted him with a message to her friend. He arrived at the knight's house on his lady's behalf... and offered him the nightingale. When the knight had listened carefully... he had a little coffer made, fashioned not of iron or steel but of pure gold ornamented with precious stones. It had a closely fitting lid. In it he placed the nightingale. Then he had the chest sealed. He carried it with him always.

Heat

In 1386 John of Gaunt, Duke of Lancaster, and the King of Portugal, led an expedition to Galicia, north-western Spain, against the King of Castile, who was supported by the French. The English troops were accompanied by noble ladies of the Duke's household.

So these two great lords and their armies were in Galicia. They stripped the country of food. The days grew hotter and hotter, until no one dared to go out riding after nine o'clock unless he wanted to be scorched by the sun... No grass could grow, nor any other eatable thing, so hard and dry and sunbaked was the earth...

The knights and squires saw how dangerous the situation might become and the shortage of foodstuffs, and the increasing strength of the sun. They began to grumble and their complaints ran through the army: 'This campaign is shaping badly... Two things tell against us particularly. We are taking women with us and they always want to sit about... This Spanish land is not a pleasant one, agreeable to campaign across as France is with all those big villages, that rich country, those cool rivers, lakes and pools, mild and palatable wines to give new strength to fighting men, and temperate climate. Everything is different here.'

The summer wore on and the sun rose higher in the sky and the days became marvellously hot. It was around mid-summer when the sun is in his strength and pride, especially in those countries of Spain and Granada and the kingdoms far from the regions of the north. Since

I Top: Infant death. Spain, fifteenth-century.   II Above: Moses before the burning bush.

the beginning of April no moisture had descended on the earth, neither rain nor dew, and the grass was burnt brown. The English ate quantities of grapes when they could get them, because they were refreshing and juicy, and then they drank those strong wines of Lisbon and Portugal to quench their thirst. But the more they drank the hotter they became, for the wines burnt their livers and lungs and all the entrails of their stomachs being quite foreign to their natural diet. The English live on mild-flavoured food and good, heavy ales, which keep their bodies humid. Now they had dry, sharp wines and drank copiously to forget their sorrows. The nights there are hot, after the heat of the previous day, but near dawn the air suddenly grows cold. This caught them unawares, for at night they could not bear to have a blanket over them and slept naked because heated by the wine. Then came the morning chill which struck through their whole bodies, giving them sickness and fever and afflicting them with dysentery, of which they inevitably died. It was the same with barons, knights and squires as with humble people.

These are the fortunes of war. It must be said that the Duke of Lancaster in Castile would never have lost so many good men in battle as died of illness in that campaign. He himself nearly died of the epidemic... out of fifteen hundred men-at-arms and a full four thousand archers whom the Duke of Lancaster had led out from England not more than half returned or even fewer.

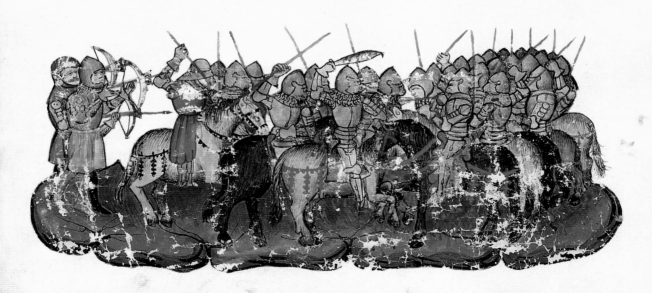

1 Top: A plague of boils.

Harvest

The Farmer's Law, a series of regulations governing rural life, was issued in the Byzantine Empire, probably in the seventh century.

60. Let those who come into another man's furrow at harvest-time and cut bundles or ears of corn or pulse be whipped and stripped of their shirts.

61. Where people enter another man's vineyard or figyard, if they come to eat, let them go unpunished; if they are there to steal, let them be beaten and stripped of their shirts.

78. If a man harvests his plot before the plots next door to his have been harvested and he brings in his beasts and they damage his neighbours' land, let him receive thirty lashes and make good the damage to the party injured.

79. If a man gathers in the fruits of his vineyard and brings in his beasts while the fruits of some plots are still ungathered, let him receive thirty lashes and make good the damage to the party injured.

1 Reaping. Queen Mary Psalter. England, early fourteenth century.

Hunger

In the fourteenth-century poem, Piers Plowman
reflects on the hunger that prevailed annually until the
first crops ripened in mid-August. (Lammas-Day is 1 August.)

'I haven't a penny left,' said Piers, 'so I can't buy you pullets or geese or
pigs. All I've got is a couple of fresh cheeses, a little curds and cream, an oat cake, and
two loaves of beans and bran which I baked for my children. Upon my soul, I haven't
a scrap of bacon, and I haven't a cook to fry you steak and onions. But I've some
parsley and shallots and plenty of cabbages, and a cow and a calf, and a mare to cart
my dung, till the drought is over. And with these few things we must live till Lammas
time, when I hope to reap a harvest in my fields. Then I can spread you a feast, as
I'd really like to.'

1 Harvesting apples. Petrus de Crescentiis, *Des profits ruraux des champs.* France, late fifteenth century.

Monks Reaping

The Spiritual Meadow from which this comes preserves a collection of moral stories put together by John Moschos, a Greek author who flourished in the late sixth and early seventh centuries.

There was an elder [monk] at Skete called David and once he went out with some other monks to reap. The Sketiotes have this custom that they go out to the estates and reap. The elder offered himself for hire on a day-to-day basis and a farmer hired him. About the sixth hour it was very hot, so the elder entered a shack and sat down. When the farmer saw him sitting there he said to him angrily: 'Elder, why are you not reaping? Don't you realise that I'm paying you?' He said: 'Yes, but the heat is so intense that the grains of wheat are falling out of the husks. I am waiting a little for the heat to abate so that you suffer no loss.' The farmer said to him: 'Get up and work, even if everything bursts into flames'... The elder stood up and suddenly the whole field began to burn. Then in fear the farmer came to the other part of the field with the elder for him to pray that the fire might cease... He offered a prayer and immediately the fire in the field was extinguished. The rest of the crop was saved. Everybody was amazed and glorified God.

I Top: Reaper. *Book of Hours*. Paris, mid-fifteenth-century.

II Above: A man sowing. *Luttrell Psalter*, English, fourteenth century.

u vilam qui agñr pme lauoit
a morue de son aue maria.

Onter vous ueu
sans nul delai:
vn miracle dun
homme lai
ou il a mit a mer
ueiller.
e t mltes genz doit esueiller
a honouuer la clere gemme

Hiring Reapers

An anonymous thirteenth-century French treatise on husbandry includes clear advice on practical matters, such as the hiring of seasonal labour for the harvest.

And you ought to know that five men can easily reap and bind two acres of any kind of corn in a day, sometimes more and other times less... You should engage the reapers as a team, that is to say five men or women, whichever you wish, and whom you term 'men', make one team and twenty-five 'men' make five teams. And twenty-five men can reap and bind ten acres a day, working full time, and in ten days one hundred acres and in twenty days two hundred acres... Ascertain how many acres there are altogether which ought to be reaped and see whether they agree with the number of working days (put down) and then allow them if correct. And if they charge you with more working days than is correct according to this calculation it should not be allowed them, because it is their fault that the proper amount has not been reaped and that they have not done the work as well as they ought to have done.

1 'The villein who could only recite one half of the Hail Mary' is shown here with his plough and oxen. He was saved by the Virgin just as he was about to be snatched up by Satan. From *The Miracles of Our Lady*, France, early thirteenth-century. The manuscript was seized at Poitiers in 1356 by the English and was brought back by Charles V who gave it to his brother, Jean de Berry.

Prayer Before an Ordeal

A prayer to bless the instruments of the ordeal.

Then the priest says this prayer: O Lord, our God, the omnipotent Father, the unfailing Light, hear us, for you are the maker of all lights. Bless O God, the fire which we have sanctified and blessed in your name, you who have illumined the whole world, that we may receive from it the light of your glory. As you did illumine Moses with the fire, so illumine our hearts and minds that we may win eternal life...

O God, the just judge, who are the author of peace and judgest with equity, we humbly beseech you so to bless this iron, which is to be used for the trial of this case, that if this

man is innocent of the charge he may take the iron in his hand, or walk upon it, without receiving harm or injury; and if he is guilty this may be made manifest upon him by your righteous power; that iniquity may not prevail over justice, nor falsehood over truth.

O Lord, the holy Father, we beseech you by the invocation of your most holy name,

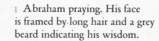

1 Abraham praying. His face is framed by long hair and a grey beard indicating his wisdom.

Prayer

The fourteenth-century mystic St Symeon of Thessaloniki on the Jesus Prayer, which is documented since the sixth century and still very widely used.

This holy prayer, the invocation of our Saviour: 'Lord Jesus Christ, Son of God, have mercy upon me,' is prayer and blessing, confession of faith and purveyor of the Holy Spirit, bringer of divine gifts and purifier of the heart, expeller of demons, indwelling of Jesus Christ, source of spiritual thoughts and godly intentions, ransomer from sin, healer of souls and bodies, conveyor of divine illumination, spring of God's mercy and crown of revelations, and gold mysteries in humility. In short, it is the only thing saving of itself, since it contains the saving name of our God, Jesus Christ, the Son of God, which is the only name we invoke, 'there is no salvation for us in any other,' as Paul says.

by the advent of your Son our Lord Jesus Christ, and by the gift of the Holy Spirit, the comforter, to bless these pieces of iron to the manifestation of your righteous judgment, that they may be so sanctified and dedicated that your truth may be made known to your faithful subjects in this trial. In the name of our Lord Jesus Christ...

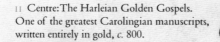

11 Centre: The Harleian Golden Gospels. One of the greatest Carolingian manuscripts, written entirely in gold, *c.* 800.

Mel.

Nature. C. et. s. mi. meltus ex eo op est in sano. Iuuamentum. ozonorificat laxat et phylet cozuptione carnu et altoz humetat noaumetum situm efficit et sititur. Remotio noaument. Cum po mis rauns.

Dil.

Health

Bartolomeo Sacchi (1421–81) wrote a treatise under the name Platina, entitled On Right Pleasure and Good Health, *in which he describes the quality of certain foodstuffs.*

On Honey

A great care and concern of bees is making honey and wax, but even greater is storing it, whence Virgil rightly calls them frugal. They do not feast like flies but are considered very clean, for no bee lights in filthy places or those which smell bad. The natural food for the bee is the rose, thyme, bee-balm, poppy, bean-blossom, the lentil, the pea, basil, and clover, for from these they gather their morning dew, from which they make honey, and flower, from which they make wax.

The best honey making is what is made from thyme, and on this account Sicilian and Attic honey bear the palm because of the abundance and sweetness of thyme. Certain authors write about Pontic and Spanish honey in which there is the force of poison, but it is pointless to discuss this when we are seeking what creates pleasure. Honey is the only substance which spits its dregs out on top; the heavier it is the better. Honey is praised differently from wine; the latter is valued because it is old and moist, the former because it is fresh and warm.

Cooked honey is considered better than raw, for it does not bloat one so much or increase pains in the midriff or bile. Summer honey is better than autumn, for it agrees with bodies which are cold and damp, heals many ills, does not allow bodies to decay, is considered best in preserving apples, gourds, citron, and nuts, and creates mouth-watering appeal in many foods.

ı Top: Caption reads: Honey
Nature: Warm and dry. *Optimum:* When it is still in the honeycomb.
Uses: It purifies, is a laxative, preserves meats, and has humidifying properties.
Dangers: Causes thirst and undergoes changes. *Neutralization of the Dangers:* With sour apples. Liege, fourteenth century.

Threshing

A seventh-century description of threshing in Anatolia from 'The Life of St Theodore of Sykeon'.

In the village of Sandos in the district of Protomeria, a certain householder, Eutolmios by name, wanted to enlarge his threshing floor because of the rich abundance of crops that had been given him and because the floor could not take a double yoke of oxen; it was close to a hillock in which there were many demons. Now as he dug and was levelling the ground in a circle round his floor he happened to dig into the neighbouring hillock and remove a stone out of it. And unclean spirits came forth and entered into the animals in the village and made them savage, and later began to work their mischief upon the villagers also... When the villagers saw the distress of their own people and thought that Eutolmios had dug in order to get money out of the hill... they grew mad against the householder and rushed to burn down him and his household... But those who held the highest positions in the village sent to the monastery begging the saint and servant of Christ, Theodore, to come and free them from the evils which had befallen them. The saint came back with them... On the morrow he made arrangements for a procession and in company with them he led the procession with prayer round the village ⁄ and the persons who were being tormented followed too ⁄ and came to the hillock which had been dug open. As he bent his head and prayed, all the spirits which had come out of it and worked mischief among the beasts and

in various places were quickly collected to that spot. The saint then turned to the afflicted and rebuked the unclean spirits that were in them. And by invocation to his master, Christ, he cast them out, and shut them all up there. After putting back the stone which had been thrown out and filling up the trench with earth, he placed above it a model of the Holy Cross, and stayed there sleepless the whole night, singing and praying to God.

I Top: Virgo, from a treatise on the signs of the zodiac.

II Above: 'Image of the lion and his ministers rejoicing, eating, drinking and celebrating.' *The Fables of the Ancients.*

Warfare

During a campaign in 882 against the Vikings, in which the Emperor Charles the Bald besieged the Norse Kings Sigifrid and Godafrid for twelve days, he succeeded in converting one of their leaders.

One day a thing remarkable for both besiegers and besieged occurred. For on July 21 in the afternoon a sudden darkness covered the whole of the sun and with thunder and lightning there was such a hailstorm that no mortal could claim to have seen anything like it before. The hailstones were not as they usually are, smooth and equal in size, but jagged and unequal and with rough edges, so that they offered to all who beheld them an unusual and extraordinary spectacle. It is remarkable and incredible to relate that they could scarcely or not at all be spanned with one's thumb and middle finger. The horses were so startled that they uprooted their tethering-posts and tore their bridles and ran around wildly and in fright both inside and outside the camps. A great part of the city which they were besieging also collapsed under the storm, so that a column in formation could have ridden in if the wall which surrounded it had not held them back. Because the siege had gone on for so many days in summer, the great army began to fall ill and be nauseated by the putrefaction of the many corpses. Those who were trapped inside were no less oppressed. There were negotiations between the two sides and it was agreed that we should give hostages, and that Sigifrid, who was stronger, should come outside the fortifications for a distance of six miles to the king. First he swore on oath that from that hour onwards as long as the Emperor Charles should live he would never again come into his kingdom to plunder it as an enemy. Then he accepted Christianity, and the emperor himself stood godfather at his baptism. They spent two days there together in joy and then our hostages were sent back from the fortification, and he contrariwise returned home with great gifts.

1 Ezekiel's vision: the siege of Jerusalem

Disguise

During civil unrest in Flanders in 1381–2, the Count of Flanders fled in disguise, having exchanged clothes with his servant, and found himself alone in the hostile city of Bruges being hunted by mercenaries.

For some time at this late hour ⁄ it was about midnight or a little after ⁄ the Count of Flanders wandered desperately through streets and alleys, until he felt forced to go into some house or other... So he entered a poor woman's house. It was no lordly manor, with halls and chambers and courtyards, but a poor grimy hovel, blackened by the smoke of the peat fire. The house consisted simply of one miserable room on the street, with an old sheet of smoke-stained cloth in it to shield the fire, and overhead a cramped little loft which was reached by a ladder with seven rungs. In the loft was a wretched bed in which the poor woman's children were sleeping.

Distraught and trembling, the Count went in and said to the woman, who was terrified at his appearance: 'Woman, save me. I am your lord the Count of Flanders. But now I must hide, my enemies are after me. If you help me, I shall reward you well.'

The poor woman recognized him, for she had often been to his door for alms... She made up her mind quickly, which was a good thing for the Count, because if she had hesitated for a moment he would have been caught talking to her by the fire. 'Sir,' she said, 'go up to the loft and get under the bed where my children are sleeping.' He did as she told him, while she stayed looking after the fire and seeing to another small child which lay in a cradle...

Then the mercenaries of Ghent arrived at the house, some of them saying that they had seen a man going in. They found the poor woman nursing her baby by the fire. 'Woman,' they asked her, 'where is the man we just saw coming in and shutting the door behind him?' 'Bless your hearts,' she replied, 'I've seen no man come in here tonight. I went out myself a few minutes ago to throw out some water, and then shut the door again. Where could I hide him? You can see all I've got here. There is my bed and my children are upstairs in another.'

One of them took a candle and went up the ladder. He poked his head into the loft and saw nothing but the little bed with the children in it. He looked round carefully and said to his comrades: 'Come on, we're wasting our time here. The woman's telling the truth. There's no one here but her and the kids.'

With this they left the house and continued their search elsewhere...
The Count of Flanders had heard the whole conversation as he lay huddled in the little bed. The state of fear he was in can be imagined. What thoughts must he have had who in the morning could say, 'I am one of the great princes of Christendom,' and that same night was reduced to such littleness? Well could he say that the chances of this world are precarious.

1 A woman wrapped in a blue-violet cloak wearing a green dress. She holds a suckling babe dressed in red. The three colours are those of the Virgin (blue, also a symbol of Christ's humanity), of love (red, for Christ's love for mankind), and of hope (green, for hope in the coming of the Messiah).

Fiesta

During the Carnival in 1464 the Constable, Don Miguel Lucas de Iranzo, organized a special fiesta in Jaén, with mummers, dances and jousts.

Then came the gardeners of the city with shields and armour and carrying great pumpkins in their hands and in the street a great tournament of pumpkins [took place], the gardeners hitting each other until there was not one pumpkin whole.

[Later in the same year] the Constable ordered a castle on wheels to be built, which was brought onto the street of Magdalen, surrounded by gardeners dressed for battle, and other men with trumpets and weapons. And a great battle ensued.

When the mobile castle reached the tower where the Constable was with his men, a great combat began [which they fought] with hard-boiled eggs against the gardeners and against each other, and between 3,000 and 4,000 eggs were used and the battle lasted for one or two hours.

ˡ 'A watcher will blow the trumpet to alert the people if he sees the sword approaching.' The text goes on to explain how people must guard themselves from sin, like those on an enemy frontier who post a man with a trumpet in a watch-tower to alert its citizens to defend themselves against the enemy. In the same way, rabbis and priests would stand in a wooden pulpit and preach often to mixed groups of Jews and Christians on the merits of following God's path, thus saving their souls.

The Trial of Joan of Arc

After her capture by the English in 1429 Joan was passed to the French authorities, who were determined to put her on trial. When they found her declarations of Christian faith to be sound, further charges were brought against her to demonstrate that she should be burnt as a witch.

Being asked whether she would take a woman's dress so that she might receive her Saviour [in communion] at Easter,

She answered that she would not leave off her dress either to receive her Saviour or for any other reason. She added that to receive her Saviour neither man's nor woman's dress made any difference; and It ought not to be refused her on account of this dress...

She admitted that at Arras and Beaurevoir she had been repeatedly asked to wear a woman's dress; which she had refused and still refuses,

And as for womanly duties,

She said there were enough other women to do them.

1 Top: Joan of Arc, in the only known contemporary likeness, sketched by the Notary of the *Paris Parlement* in the margin of the official history of the siege of Orleans.

Ceremony of Marriage

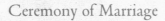

The epic poem, The Ruodlieb, dating from the mid-eleventh century, is written in medieval Latin although it describes courtly society in the Germanic lands, with dramatic accounts of adventures both abroad and at home. Here, the hero Ruodlieb presides over a marriage ceremony.

Then Ruodlieb... said that it was agreed by all relations and friends that this youth and this girl were burning with love for one another. They all asked him if he wished to take her as his wife, and with a smile on his face he replied, 'I do.' Then they asked her if she for her part wished willingly to take him as her lord; she too smiled a little, and then said, 'Should I not want a slave vanquished in a game, whom I beat at dice with this agree-ment as our stake, that whether he won or whether he lost he should marry only me? I want him to serve me with all his might both night and day, and the better he does this, the dearer he shall be to me.' Then there was a tremendous roar of laughter from everyone, because she had spoken so brazenly and yet in such a friendly way. When they saw that her mother did not oppose these things and that the families of both were well-matched in status and wealth, they took counsel and decided that they were well suited to one another, and that she should be betrothed to him in a lawful bond.

The bridegroom drew his sword and scraped it along the stonework. A gold ring was fixed onto its hilt, and the bride-groom offered it to his bride, saying to her, 'As this ring encircles the whole of your finger all around, so I bind my faith to you firmly and forever, and you must observe it towards me, or lose your head.' She very wittily gave him the apt reply, 'It is fitting for both to suffer the same judgment: why must I keep better faith towards you than you towards me?... When you went off wenching, would you have liked me to be a whore for you? May it not be that I should be joined to you on this condition; be off with you, farewell, you may go wenching as much as you wish, but not with me. There are plenty in the world whom I can wed as well as you.' So saying, she left him his sword and his ring. The young man said to her, 'Let it be done as you wish, darling. If I ever do this, let me lose the goods I gave you, and let you have the right to cut off this head of mine.' A smile passed over her lips as she turned back to him and said, 'Let us be joined now on those terms, with no deceit.' Her suitor said 'Amen' to this and kissed her. When they were thus united the people gave a roar of approval and praising God, they sang a wedding hymn.

Jews of Babylonia

Benjamin of Tudela set out from Saragossa, Spain, in 1160 to visit Jewish communities throughout the Near East and Persia, including Baghdad.

Bagdad contains about one thousand Jews, who enjoy peace, comfort and much honour under the government of the great king... The principal of all these... is Daniel, the son of Chisdei, who bears the titles of Prince of the Captivity and Lord, and who possesses a pedigree which proves his descent from King David. The Jews call him 'Lord, Prince of the Captivity', and the Mahometans entitle him Saidna Ben Daoud, noble descendent of David... The Emir-al-Mumenin, the lord of the Mahometans, has... confirmed his power by granting him a seal of office... All the Jewish congregations receive authority from the prince of the captivity to elect rabbis and ministers, all of whom appear before him in order to receive consecration and the permission to officiate... The prince of the captivity possesses hostelries, gardens, and orchards in Babylonia, and extensive landed property inherited from his fore-fathers, of which nobody can deprive him... He is very rich, an excellent scholar, and so hospitable that numerous Israelites dine at his table.

Many of the Jews of Bagdad are good scholars and very rich. The city contains twenty-eight synagogues, situated partly in Bagdad and partly in Al-Khorkh, on the other side of the river Tigris, which runs through and divides the city. The metropolitan synagogue of the prince of the captivity is ornamented with pillars of richly coloured marble, plated with gold and silver; on the pillars are inscribed verses of the Psalms in letters of gold. The ascent to the holy ark is composed of ten marble steps, on the uppermost of which are the stalls set apart for the prince of the captivity and the other princes of the house of David.

[I] Jewish wedding scenes. Northern Italy, after 1450.

[II] The scroll of the Law, draped in red and gold damask, is removed by a Jew from the Ark for a Festival or Sabbath morning ceremony. Italy, *c.* 1479.

Difficult Choices

*In this anonymous twelfth-century Provençal poem,
two young girls ask Lady Carenza for her advice on
marriage and are recommended to devote themselves to
Coronat de Scienza, the Crown of Knowledge, i.e. God.*

Na Carenzat al bel cors avinen

Alais: Lady Carenza, you of the graceful and lovely body,
                 give counsel to us two sisters.
           And since you know best how to sift over the best,
                 counsel me according to your own wisdom.
                 Shall I take a husband from among our
                        acquaintance?
           or remain a virgin? That would please me,
           since I don't think much of having babies,
           and being married seems too depressing to me.

Iselda: Lady Carenza, having a husband would agree with me,
                 but I think having babies is a great penance.
                 Your breasts hang right down to the ground
                 and your belly is burdensome and annoying.

Carenza: Lady Alais and Lady Iselda, you have a good education,
                 reputation and beauty, youth and fresh colour,
                 you have understanding, courtesy, and merit
                 above all the other ladies of my acquaintance.
           For this reason I counsel you, in order to get good seed,
                 take Coronat de Scienza for your husband,
           From him you'll have the fruit of glorious children.
                 Those who marry him remain virgins...

I The birth of Alexander. *Livre des fais d 'Alexandre le grant.* Bruges, *c.* 1475.

Cy commence le premier liure assamble de pluseurs et adiouste aux
histoires de quintecurse Ruffe lequel contient xxxiij. chapitres
Dont le premier parle comment es histoires dalexandre puelt ap
paroir que les roiaulmes croissent p vertu de dilligence et declinent
par vicieuse laschete. Et preuue que alexandre conquist toute la
partie dorient

Regardant
les discordes
et Infeliatez
des roiaulmes
et seigneurie

Et voulant aussi moustrer que
en leurs malheuretez a tort se
excusent les rois ou princes
sur faulte de bon peuple. Et

ad missas bte virginis offinz
alne sancta parē
cuica puerpa regē
qui cclii terriq. re
git i scla sector. R.
post partu vgo i
molata pmansist[e
dei gcnitric intercede pro nob. Slona

An Artist's Vision

In eleventh-century London, a painter by the name of Teodwin was scourged because he dared to work on the holy day of Bishop Erkenwald.

During the period when the body of the holy prelate was still being kept in its coffin in the crypt, the vault of the crypt had to be painted. Now Erkenwald's festival took place while this was going on, but on this particular day mass was not being celebrated there... on account of the erection of the scaffolding the painter needed for his work.

However, a great crowd of people of both sexes, who wished to pray, assembled at the oratory bearing offerings and candles. But they were denied entrance. For the painter had barred the door and carried on painting the curve of the vault with his paint and dyes.

While he was painting away, with great industry, however, he was all at once bereft of his strength and, gripped by a sudden pain, he fell to the ground as if his life had left him.

When he suffered this for a long time, sleep enveloped him and lo, the aforesaid prelate, garbed in his episcopal regalia, came to him and beat him hard with his pastoral staff, reminding him how disrespectful he had been to persist in working on that day and to lock people out...

After he had recovered from his illness, he made known to many people this vision and chastisement.

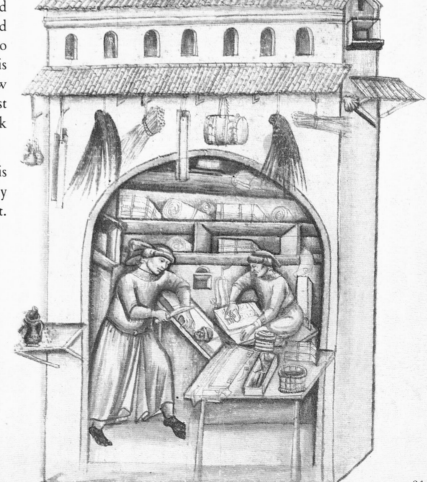

I Opposite page: Medieval congregation and organist from the Prayer Book of King Alphonso V of Aragon, 1442.

II Right: The preparation of parchment was an art. Parchment was extremely expensive and only the most important works were executed on 'fresh' parchment. Others were written on palimpsests where the original writing was erased so that the parchment could be reused. This parchment maker's shop is from Floriano da Villola's Chronicle, Italy.

Artistic Techniques

In the first half of the twelfth century, 'Theophilus' produced a very detailed treatise on the techniques used in artistic production of the time. He was probably Roger of Helmarshausen, a skilled metalworker and Benedictine monk, and he addresses his readers thus:

Wherefore, dearest son ∕ be eager and anxious to look at this little work... You will find in it whatever kinds and blends of various colours Greece possesses; whatever Russia knows of workmanship in enamels or variety of niello: whatever Arabia adorns with repoussé or cast work, or engravings in relief: whatever gold embellishments Italy applies to various vessels or to the carving of gems and ivories: whatever France esteems in her precious variety of windows: whatever skilled Germany praises in subtle work in gold, silver, copper, iron, wood and stone...

There are many kinds of gold, of which the best derives from the land of Havilah... When men, skilled in this art, find veins of it in the ground, they dig them up and, when it has been refined in the fire and proved in the furnace, make use of it for their own purposes. There is also a very precious Arabian gold, which is of an exceptional red colour. It is frequently found used in antique vases. Modern workmen counterfeit its appearance by adding a fifth part of red copper to pale gold, and they deceive many unwary people. This can be guarded against in this way. The gold is put in the fire and, if it is pure, it does not lose its brightness. If, however, it is adulterated, it completely changes colour.

There is also gold, called Spanish gold, which is prepared from red copper, powder of basilisk and human blood and vinegar... There is another gold, called sand gold, which is found on the banks of the Rhine in this way. The sand is dug up in those places where one expects to find it, and is placed on wooden boards. Then water is repeatedly and carefully poured over it. The sand flows away, and very fine gold remains, which is put in a vessel by itself. When the vessel is half full, quicksilver is added, and is vigorously worked with the hand until the contents are completely mixed together. This is placed in a fine cloth, the quicksilver is squeezed out and what remains is placed in a crucible and melted.

I 'Unless the Lord builds the house, those who build it labour in vain'. Psalm 129, Italy, *c.* 1280.

II Opposite page: Alchemists from Thomas Norton's *Ordinal of Alchemy*. England, *c.* 1490.

The Elephant

In the anonymous fourteenth-century Byzantine story,
Entertaining Tales of Quadrupeds, *King Lion summons all*
the beasts in 1364 to introduce their merits. Each makes fun
of the others until at the end they give up peaceful debate
and a battle royal breaks up the gathering.

The elephant then came to centre stage,
and he addressed the whole assembly thus:
'Just like a tower, safe and fortified,
a fort impregnable, firm to the end,
thus too stand I, robust beyond compare.
Thus bastions are built on me, made of boards,
and solid towers, also, out of wood,
soundly fortified. Soldiers in those towers
stand resolute, fiercely combat their foes,
and overpower and defeat them all.

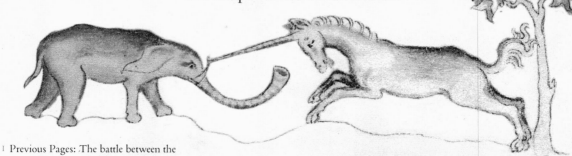

1 Previous Pages: The battle between the
Great Khan's marshal and the King of Mien.

Also my tusks are put to many uses:
in royal beds, and seats of patriarchs,
and thrones of emperors, and queens as well,
and in carved staffs, with jewel settings lathed,
for metropolitans to hold, and bishops,
and for head abbots with their beards so long.
The noblemen and merchants use them, too,
for games they own: lathed chess-pieces and chessboards,
backgammon boards, and all things of the sort.
They make knife-handles, too, for fine, long knives,
as well as the exquisite smaller ones;
and very pretty combs, all bound in gold,
and wrought with silver and with emeralds,
which noblemen possess, both young and old.
The young lads use these combs to comb their hair;
they comb that long blond hair they often have.
Blonde ladies of the court and noble dames
will also comb their hair and their blond tresses;
and ladies of the court adjust their partings.
Young girls, it must be said, will part their hair,
as do blonde damsels, to look fair and decent.
They even use my tusks to frame those glasses,
or mirrors, as they're known, in which young lasses
gaze on their image. Such, then, are the merits
and the advantages that I enjoy.'

II Top left:
A dragon coiled
around an elephant
from the *Aberdeen
Bestiary*. English,
twelfth-century.

III Kublai Khan
leaves to hunt for
gyrfalcons. *Livre des
Merveilles*, written
at the beginning
of the fifteenth
century, recounting
the story of Marco
Polo's travels.

The Cock and the Wolf

In the late eighth and early ninth century, the Anglo-Saxon scholar, Alcuin, was in residence at the court of Charlemagne and reworked the familiar fable of 'The Cock and the Wolf'.

There is a bird called by the special surname, 'cock'. This bird announces day-break, dispels shadows from the earth, marks the times of the day, and is girded in his loins. The flock of chickens is ruled subject to his authority...

Oh what a sorrow! A barrier of roads once constrained him as he was hastening a long way off, testing for food with his beak. Therefore, as he seeks food by himself and ranges over the crossroads, alas! Boasting, too bold and very proud, he is snatched by the lurking wolf.

Oppressed by this burden, the cock at once finds for himself this scheme for escaping: 'Often your fame, O wolf of exceeding strength, has come to my ears and has told me in a strange rumour that your great voice can produce a deep sound with bright harmonies. I do not grieve so much to be devoured by a hated mouth as to be cheated of being allowed to learn from you what was possible to believe about your voice.'

The beast put credence in what was said, and the wolf, swollen with love of the praise that had been offered, opens his hellish throat, spreads wide his gluttonous jaws, and unlocks the innermost chamber of the vast cavern.

But swiftly the bird, harbinger of daybreak, is rescued, and in a bound flies and quickly clings to a tree branch. As soon as he has gained sudden freedom, the bird sitting on high brings forth songs with these words: 'Whoever grows proud without reason is deservedly deceived, and whoever is taken in by false praise will go without food, so long as he tries to spread about empty words before eating.'

Top: 'Image of the cock speaking and composing fables against the hawk.' *The Fable of the Ancients,* a book of moral tales full of witticisms and double entendres, written in verse in 1281 by Isaac Ibn Sahula.

Prayer

St Francis of Assisi, the founder of the Franciscan order, who died in 1226, was particularly famous for his inspiring preaching and vernacular hymns.

Where there is love and wisdom,
there is neither fear nor ignorance.
Where there is patience and humility,
there is neither anger nor annoyance.
Where there is poverty and joy,
there is neither cupidity nor avarice.
Where there is peace and contemplation,
    there is neither care nor restlessness.
        Where fear of the Lord guards the house,
            there no enemy can enter.

Where there is mercy and prudence, there is neither excess nor harshness.

I Ad Vesperas. Scene from the Life of Mary.

A Miraculous Statue

Little is known about Master Gregory, author of this piece. He may have been English and appears to have visited Rome in the thirteenth century.

There was in Rome an incredible wonder, an iron statue of Bellerophon and his horse, positioned in mid air, neither suspended from above by any chain nor supported by any post beneath. You see, the vault had an arc of magnetic stones on each side, which attracted the statue proportionately from different directions, and thus it remained balanced. Its weight was thought to be about 15,000 pounds of iron.

II The Horse and the naked figure of Hercules as if in flight, carrying a club and a lion's skin. Both from a manuscript *Hyginus, De astronomia*, written and illuminated in Padua, fifteenth-century.

The twelfth century Pilgrim's Guide *to the route to Compostela describes the four common routes and the sights and dangers encountered along the way.*

On leaving that country [of Gascony], to be sure on the road of St James, there are two rivers that flow near the village of Saint-Jean-de-Sorde, one to the right and one to the left, and of which one is called brook and the other river. There is no way of crossing them without a raft. May their ferrymen be damned! Though each of the streams is indeed quite narrow, they have the habit of demanding one coin from each man, whether poor or rich, whom they ferry over, and for a horse they ignominiously extort by force four. Now, their boat is small, made of a single tree, hardly capable of holding horses. Also, when boarding it one must be most careful not to fall by chance into the water. You will do well in pulling your horse by the reins behind yourself in the water, outside the boat, and to embark but with few passengers, for if it is overloaded it will soon become endangered...

Then, already near the pass of Cize, one reaches the Basque country, on the seashore of which, towards the north, lies the city of Bayonne. This land, whose language is barbarous, is wooded, mountainous, devoid of bread, wine, and all sorts of food for the body, except that, in compensation, it abounds in apples, cider, and milk.

In this land, that is to say near Port-de-Cize in the town called Ostabat and in those of Saint-Jean and Saint-Michel-Pied-de-Port, there are evil toll-gatherers who will certainly be damned through and through. In point of fact, they actually advance towards the pilgrims with two or three sticks, extorting by force an unjust tribute. And if some traveller refuses to hand over the money at their request, they beat him with the sticks and snatch away the toll-money while cursing him and searching even through his breeches. These are ferocious people... and their barbarous speech scares the wits out of those who see them.

Travel

Benjamin of Tudela set out from Saragossa, Spain, in 1160 and travelled throughout the Near East and Persia to the frontiers of China, visiting Baghdad.

Bagdad [sic] is the large metropolis of the Calif Emir-al Mumenin al Abassi, of the family of their prophet, who is the chief of the Mahometan religion. All Mahometan kings acknowledge him, and he holds the same dignity over them which the Pope enjoys over the Christians... This great Abbaside is extremely friendly towards the Jews, many of his officers being of that nation; he understands all languages, is well versed in the Mosaic law, and reads and writes the Hebrew tongue... The calif leaves his palace but once every year, namely, at the time of the feast called Ramadan; on which occasion many visitors assemble from distant parts, in order to have an opportunity of beholding his countenance. He then bestrides the royal mule, dressed in kingly robes, which are composed of gold and silver cloth. On his head he wears a turban, ornamented with precious stones of inestimable value; but over this turban is thrown a black veil, as a sign of humility, and as much as to say: 'See all this worldly honour will be converted into darkness on the day of death.'

He is accompanied by a numerous retinue of Mahometan nobles, arrayed in rich dresses and riding upon horses, princes of Arabia, of Media, or Persia, and even of Tibet, a country distant three months' journey from Arabia... All who walk in procession, both men and women, are dressed in silk and purple... The procession moves on into the court of the mosque, where the calif mounts a wooden pulpit and expounds their law unto them. The learned Mahometans rise, pray for him, and praise his great kindness and piety; upon which the whole assembly answers, 'Amen!' The calif then pronounces his blessing, and kills a camel, which is led thither for that purpose, and this is their offering...

The city of Bagdad is three miles in circumference; the country in which it is situated is rich in palm-trees, gardens, and orchards, so that nothing equals it in Mesopotamia. Merchants of all countries resort thither for purposes of trade, and it contains many wise philosophers, well skilled in sciences, and magicians proficient in all sorts of enchantment.

Sultan Sanjar and the old woman from a Persian manuscript written in Baghdad in 1396

The Swan

In his catalogue of birds, Hugh of Fouilloy, who died in 1172/3, often quotes from ancient authorities. Here he prefaces his entry on the swan by a quotation from Isidore of Seville, whose seventh-century Etymologies *was considered an encyclopaedia of accurate information.*

'The swan is named surely for its singing, because with melodious notes it gives forth a sweet song. Moreover, it [is said] to sing so sweetly because it has a long and curving neck, and it is inevitable that a voice forcing its way through a long and flexible passage will produce various melodies. It is reported that many swans fly to the singing lyricists in the northern regions, and join properly in the mode.'

The swan has snowy plumage, but black skin. Allegorically the snowy colour of plumage denotes the effect of the pretence by which the black flesh is hidden, because a sin of the flesh is veiled by pretence. While the swan swims in the river it carries its neck erect, because a proud man who is enticed by worldly possessions also at the same time prides himself in possession of transitory things.

'It is reported that many swans fly to the singing lyricists in the northern regions, and join properly in the mode,' because those who covet pleasures with all their hearts harmonize with pleasure seekers as if flying to them. But at the last, when the swan is dying, it is said to sing exceedingly sweetly as it dies. Likewise, when the proud man departs this life, he delights still in the sweetness of this world, and dying, he remembers the things which he did wrong.

I 'Image of the cock showing his broken wing to the partridge and to all members of the party.' *Fables of the Ancients*, a moralistic book written in 1281 by Isaac Ibn Sahula and copied here in the fifteenth-century in Italy.

II Top: The swan from one of the most dramatic of all bestiaries. Latin, 1230-40.

But when the swan is deprived of its snowy plumage, set on a spit, it is roasted at a fire.
Likewise, when at death the wealthy, proud man is stripped of his worldly glory, descending
to the flames of hell, he will be punished with torments, and he who
was accustomed to seek nourishment in the lowest quarters,
descending into the abyss, becomes food for the fire.

III The 'swan' constellation,
from the *Phaenomena* of Aratus.
Carolingian, ninth-century.

Ambassadors

Liutprand of Cremona was twice ambassador to Byzantium and left a detailed account of his first trip in 949 when he represented Berengar, ruler of Italy, to Constantine VII (913–59).

On the first of August [949] I left Pavia and sailing down the Po arrived in three days at Venice. There I met a Greek envoy, the eunuch Salemo, chamberlain of the palace, who had just returned from Spain and Saxony. He was anxious to sail for Constantinople and was taking there with him [another envoy]... a rich merchant of Maintz called Liutefred... who was the bearer of costly presents. Finally, we left Venice on the twenty-fifth of August and reached Constantinople on the seventeenth of September. It will be a pleasant task to describe the marvellous and unheard of manner of our reception.

Next to the imperial residence at Constantinople there is a palace of remarkable size and beauty which the Greeks called Magnavra... the name being equivalent to 'Fresh Breeze'. In order to receive some Spanish envoys, who had recently arrived, as well as myself and Liutefred, Constantine [the emperor] gave orders that this palace should be got ready and the following preparations made.

Before the emperor's seat stood a tree, made of bronze gilded over, whose branches were filled with birds, also made of gilded bronze, which uttered different cries, each according to its species. The throne itself was so marvellously fashioned that at one moment it seemed a low structure, and at another it rose high into the air. It was of immense size and was guarded by lions made either of bronze or of wood covered over with gold, who beat the ground with their tails and gave a dreadful roar with open mouth and quivering tongue. Leaning upon the shoulders of two eunuchs I was brought into the emperor's presence. At my approach the lions began to roar and the birds to cry out... but I was neither terrified nor surprised, for I had previously made enquiry about all these things from people who were well acquainted with them. So after I had three times made obeisance to the emperor with my face upon the ground, I lifted my head, and behold! The man whom just before I had seen sitting on a moderately elevated seat had now changed his raiment and was sitting on the level of the ceiling. How it was done I could not imagine, unless perhaps he was lifted up by some such sort of device as we use for raising the timbers of a wine press...

1 Opposite page: Solomon's throne. The text of the Ten Commandments in Castilian is written on the steps of the throne.

Prayer for a Soul in Purgatory

Jacobus de Voragine included in his collection of saints' lives,
The Golden Legend, *several stories used as examples (exempla).*
In this one he demonstrates how prayers said by the living can aid
the dead who languish in Purgatory.

Souls can reveal to the living their misery and obtain from them
offerings that will shorten their penalty. Thus we read that the

fishers of Saint Theobald, while fishing in the autumn, caught in their nets a huge block of ice instead of fish, which pleased them more than if they had caught fishes because their bishop was suffering from pains in his feet and by applying this ice to them they would offer him a refreshing relief. But at a certain moment the bishop heard a voice coming from the ice. And when he begged the voice to identify itself, it said, 'I am a soul, imprisoned in this ice for my sins; I may be delivered if you say thirty masses for me on thirty successive days without interruption.'

The bishop had said half of this series of masses and prepared himself for the next mass when at the instigation of the devil a violent quarrel broke out in the city, which involved nearly all the inhabitants. So the bishop was called to put down the disorder; he took off his sacred vestments and could not say the mass that day. So he had to begin again from the beginning and had already accomplished two-thirds of the series when a vast army appeared to besiege the city. He was obliged to interrupt the series of masses. He began again; he had said all the masses except the last one when the palace and the bishop's property seemed about to burn down. His servants told him to interrupt the mass but he refused saying, 'Even if the whole property has to burn down, I would finish saying this mass.' The celebration was thus achieved, the ice melted immediately, and the fire which all thought they had seen straightway disappeared like a ghost, without causing the slightest damage...

Michael wins victory over Satan with Gabriel at his side. A group of men cover their eyes while Daniel, their leader, points with his forefinger. A hand stretches out towards them from a cloud, symbolising divine intervention. The scene represents the end of iniquity and the advent of eternal justice.

101

The Feast of St Demetrios

A twelfth-century Byzantine text, called Timarion *after its hero, preserves an account of a visit to Thessaloniki at the time of the festival of St Demetrios (8 October).*

After we had visited the most sacred and holy places, where we paid the appropriate respects, we spent some time at the fair that was set up outside the city gates... The fair is the most important held in Macedonia. Not only does the native and indigenous throng pour in but also men of every conceivable race and country...

I myself, being just a Cappadocian tourist from abroad... wanted to see everything there was to see at the same time, to make sure I didn't miss a thing. So I climbed up a hill overlooking the fair where I could sit down and observe everything at leisure. And this is what there was. There were merchants' booths facing each other, set up in parallel rows. These rows extended for a long way and were far enough apart to form a walkway in the middle that was wide enough to allow space to move for the teeming crowd. Looking at the closeness of the booths and the evenness of their positioning, you could compare them to lines drawn over a long distance from two opposite points. At various points at an angle to the rows, other booths were set up. They were in rows as well, not long ones, but like the tiny feet that grow alongside reptiles' coils... I couldn't help but compare it to the centipede with a very long body showing innumerable little feet under its belly.

And... there were all kinds of men's and women's clothes both woven and spun, everything that comes from Boeotia and the Peloponnese, and all the things that merchant ships bring from Italy and Greece. Phoenicia also supplies many goods, as do Egypt, Spain, and the Pillars of Hercules, where the finest altar cloths are made. These items the merchants export directly from their respective countries to old Macedonia and Thessalonica. The Black Sea also contributes to the fair by sending across its own products to Constantinople, from where they are conveyed by large numbers of horses and mules...

When I had had a good long look at all of this... I went back into the city very keen to see other things, above all the sacred gathering.

I Opposite page: The fortified town in the centre of the illustration is probably Constantinople while it was still in Christian hands. The Golden Horn and the Bosphorus appear in the miniature, while in the foreground, palm trees mix incongruously with bulrushes.

II Above: An icon of St Demetrios holding a lance and shield. The cross was added at a later date. The tall, slender figure of the young warrior, painted around 1500, is in the tradition of the thin, elongated warrior saints of the fourteenth and fifteenth centuries.

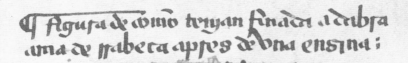

A Cunning Escape

Anna Komnene, daughter of Emperor Alexios I, mistrusted the Norman leader Bohemund (c. 1050/8—1111), who participated in the First Crusade. As an instance of his trickery, she reported the way he escaped from Antioch by feigning his own death.

When Bohemund had neither an army on land nor a fleet at sea; and danger menaced him from both sides... he devised a plan which was exceedingly sordid, and yet exceedingly ingenious. [He] had a report spread about himself, which said that Bohemund had died, and when he found that it had taken good hold, a wooden coffin was soon prepared and a bireme, in which the coffin was placed, and also he, the living corpse, sailed away from... Antioch, to Rome. Thus Bohemund was carried across the sea as a corpse, for to all appearance he was a corpse to judge by the coffin and the demeanour of his companions (for wherever they stopped the barbarians plucked out their hair and mourned him ostentatiously), and inside he was lying stretched out dead for the time being, but for the rest inhaling and exhaling air through unseen holes. This took place at the sea-ports; but when the boat was out at sea, they gave him food and attention; and then afterwards the same lamentations and trickeries were repeated. And to make the corpse appear stale and odoriferous, they strangled or killed a cock and placed it with the corpse. And when a cock has been dead for four or five days its smell is most disagreeable for those who have a sense of smell. And this smell seemed to those who are deceived by outward appearance to be that of Bohemund's body; and that villain Bohemund enjoyed this fictitious evil all the more.

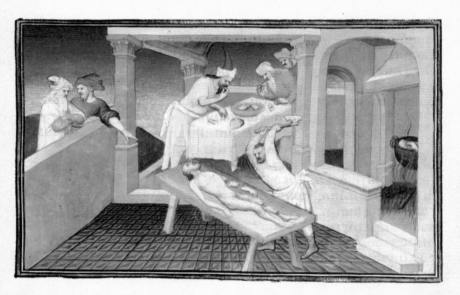

When he reached Corfu... and was now safe, he arose from the dead and left the corpse-bearing coffin there and basked in more sunlight and breathed purer air and wandered about the town of Corfu. And the inhabitants seeing him in his foreign and barbaric garb asked his lineage and his fortune, and who he was, whence he came and to whom he was going. However, he treated them all with contempt...

I Above: Cannibals on the Andaman Islands

II A section of the Mappa Mundi by Abraham Cresques of Majorca, 1375. One of the best complete maps of the period, inspired in part by Marco Polo's travel journal, it gave a physical, economic, political, historical and mythological description of his time.

Fiesta

An old German proverb.

No play without fools!

The Autumn of Life

From the Carmina Burana, *a collection of songs made in the twelfth century.*

While life's April blossom blew,
What I willed I then might do,
Lust and law seemed comrades true.
　As I listed, unresisted,
Hither, thither, could I play,
And my wanton flesh obey.

When life's autumn days decline,
Thus to live, a libertine,
Fancy-free as thoughts incline,
　Manhood's older age and colder
Now forbids; removes, destroys
All those ways of wonted joys.

Age with admonition wise
Thus doth counsel and advise,
While her voice within me cries:
　For repenting and relenting
There is room; forgiveness falls
On all contrite prodigals.

I will seek a better mind;
Change, correct, and leave behind
What I did with purpose blind:
　From vice sever, with endeavour
Yield my soul to serious things,
Seek the joy that virtue brings.

I Opposite page: Sobriety; Gluttony; A Frugal Meal; Dives and Lazarus. Frère Laurent, La Somme le roi. France, *c.* 1294.

II Above: 'Image of the astrologers, two and two they came and were hid in prison houses.' *Fables of the Ancients*, a book of Hebrew morality copied here in a fifteenth-century miscellany.

III Top right: 'Image of the fool behaving strangely'

IV Above: 'Image of the Interlocutor and the author, speaking to each other.'

Autumn

An anonymous Hebrew poem on the coming of autumn, written in Spain between the ninth and eleventh centuries.

The days of summer are gone. The rainy season is here. Its showers will gather, then pour themselves, more and more, upon the earth. Grain, wine, and oil will flourish quickly. The clouds will send down rain, and urge the earth to bring forth grass. Seeds and buds will grow in beauty. Voices of thunder will herald: 'Those who sow in tears shall reap with songs of joy!'

I Above: The text contains a warning that autumn may be harmful to people with a tendency towards melancholy.

II Opposite page: Preparation of linen which is said to moderate the heat of the body and can be used to dry up ulcerations.

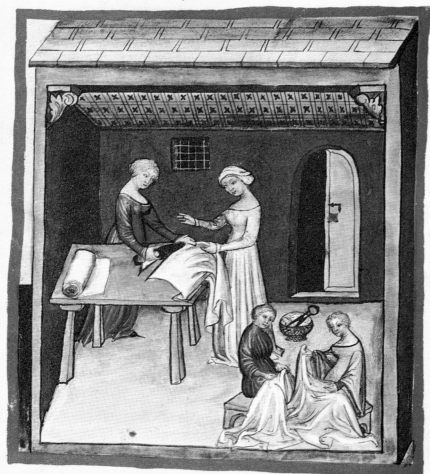

The Miracle of the Bloody Shirt

In 862 the anonymous chronicler associated with the monastery of St Bertin recorded this event, which persuaded the bishop to establish the Feast of the Virgin's Assumption in Thérouanne.

Meanwhile a miracle occurred at Thérouanne. On the morning of the day of Mary's Assumption [15 August], the slave-woman of a certain citizen of that town began to iron a linen garment, the sort called in the vulgar tongue a shirt, so that it would be all ready for her master to wear when he went to mass. The first time she put the iron down on it and pushed it across it, the shirt became stained with blood. And so it went on: whenever the slave put the iron across, blood followed it, until the whole garment was quite dyed in the blood pressed on to it. Hunfrid, the venerable bishop of that town, had the shirt brought to him and kept in the church as witness to the miracle. Because the feast of Mary's Assumption had not previously been celebrated by the inhabitants of his diocese, he gave orders that this solemn occasion should be celebrated by all and kept as a feast with due reverence.

1 This map compresses a great deal of information into a small area ⁄ it is less than 10 centimetres across ⁄ and is related to the large Ebstorf and Hereford maps. Like them, it has Jerusalem at the centre, while depicted along the right-hand edge are a series of monstrous races.

Jerusalem Fair

In the late seventh century, Adamnan, Abbot of the monastery of Iona in western Scotland, wrote down an account by Bishop Arculf of his pilgrimage to the Holy Land.

On the twelfth day of the month of September... there is an annual custom whereby a huge concourse of people from various nations everywhere is wont to come together in Jerusalem to do business by mutual buying and selling. Consequently it happens inevitably that crowds of different peoples are lodged in this hospitable city for some days. Owing to the very great number of their camels, horses, asses, and oxen, all carriers of divers merchandise, filth from their discharges spreads everywhere throughout the city streets, the stench proving no little annoyance to the citizens, and walking being impeded. Wonderful to relate, on the night of the day on which the said bands depart with their various beasts of burden, there is released from the clouds an immense downpour of rain, which descends on the city, and renders it clean of dirt by purging away all the abominable filth from the streets... The flood of heavenly waters, then, pouring through the eastern gates, and bearing all the filth and nuisance with it, enters the valley of Josaphat, swells the torrent of Cedron, and after such a baptism of Jerusalem straightway the copious flood ceases.

Thus one should carefully note the magnitude and character of the honour which this chosen and famous city has in the sight of the eternal father, who does not suffer it to remain soiled for long, but quickly cleanses it out of reverence for his only begotten son, who has the honoured places of his holy cross and resurrection within the compass of its walls.

Pagans

Liutprand, appointed Bishop of Cremona in 962, chronicled the violent attacks of the pagan Hungarians who threatened central, eastern and western Europe.

King Henry [of Saxony] was laid up with a serious illness when he was informed of the Hungarians' near approach. He scarcely waited for the report to end but sent off messengers at once through Saxony, bidding every man who could come to him in five days under pain of death. Before the time had expired a strong army had assembled; for it is the laudable and praiseworthy custom of the Saxons to allow no male above the age of thirteen to shirk military service... A flying messenger rushed in with news that the Hungarians were at Merseburg, a castle on the borders of the Saxons, Thuringians and Slavonians. He added that they had taken a huge company of women and children prisoners and had killed an immense number of men; for they had declared, in order to strike terror into the Saxons, that they would leave no one over ten years of age alive. The king's firm courage, however, was not dismayed, but he urged his men all the more vehemently to battle, telling them it was their bounden duty to fight for their country and meet a glorious end...

The battle began immediately. From the Christians' ranks on all sides was heard the holy, and wonderous cry, 'Kyrie eleison' 'Lord have mercy upon us': from the heathen came the foul and diabolical shout 'Hui Hui'.

Before the beginning of the engagement Henry had given his men this sagacious and practical advice: 'When you are hastening forward to the first skirmish, let no one of you try to get ahead of his comrades just because he has a swifter horse. Cover yourselves on one side with your bucklers, and catch the first flight of arrows on your shields: then rush at them at full speed as furiously as you can, so that before they have time to fire a second volley they may feel the blows of our swords upon their heads.' The Saxons accordingly... advanced in level line. No one used his horse's speed to get in front of his slower neighbour, but covering themselves on one side with their shields... they caught the enemies' arrows on them and rendered them harmless. Then... they rushed at full speed upon the foe, who groaned and gave up the ghost before they could shoot again. So, by the kindness of God's grace, the Hungarians found flight preferable to battle. Their swiftest horses then seemed sluggish to them: their gorgeous trappings and bright shields appeared a burden rather than a protection. They threw aside their bows, flung away their arrows, tore off their horses' trappings, that nothing might check their speed, and thought of nothing but precipitate flight. But Almighty God, who had stripped them of courage for the fray, denied them any chance of escape. The Hungarians accordingly were cut to pieces and put to flight, the great throng of their prisoners was released, and the voice of lamentation changed to songs of joy.

I Above right: Joshua slays the kings vanquished by the Israelites.

II Opposite page: The defence of Jerusalem's walls while they are under reconstruction. The defenders of Jerusalem, with a weapon in one hand and a rod in the other, illustrate the fact that the builders had to keep one hand free at all times to defend themselves.

The Effects of Wine

Verses on the perils of drinking wine from Juan Ruiz's The Book of Good Love.

Excessive drinking shortens life and makes
the vision faint;
It takes the vital force away if drunk
without restraint;
It makes the members tremble and it gives the
mind a taint;
Indeed, with every bottle comes another new complaint.

But worst of all it fouls the breath by causing halitosis,
And science yet has found no cure for such a diagnosis,
Besides, it burns the gut and wastes the liver with cirrhosis
So, if you will succeed in love, take wine in smaller doses.

I A youth takes a ripe grape from a bunch he has just picked from the vine.

II A husband and wife sit together at a festive table. He drinks his fill while his young bride looks on.

III Opposite page: The four wives of the Great Khan and their sons, *Livre des Merveilles*, early fifteenth century, France.

A Warning Against Wine

From a question-and-answer dialogue attributed to Bede come these words of wisdom.

Better to study for one hour with the wise than to drink
wine with the foolish!

An Auspicious Birth

This is Gerald of Wales' account of the birth of a male heir to the French throne in 1165. The child, Philip Augustus, would rule from 1180 to 1223.

I think I should not pass over a thing which befell the writer of these words. When in the years of his youth he was devoting himself most zealously to the study of the liberal arts at Paris, it came to pass that at the beginning of autumn, about the first sleep when the night was yet young, the said Philip was by the grace of God born of his mother's womb. And when the fame thereof was heard in the city and received with joy inexpressible by human speech through the whole of that great city there was such a sound and clanging of bells and such a multitude of tapers were kindled through all the open places of the town, that not knowing what such a sound and unwonted tumult might mean together with such a blaze of light by night, men deemed that the city was threatened by a great conflagration. Wherefore the author of this work, a stripling living in the city and then near the completion of his twentieth year, was awakened from the bed on which he had just fallen asleep and looking forth beheld in the place without, two women old and very poor, but none the less carrying tapers in their hands and showing great joy in their faces and in every movement of their bodies running with hasty steps to meet each other as though they would dash one against the other. And when he asked them for the cause of such commotion and rejoicing, one of them looked back at him and thus made answer: 'We have a King now given us by God, an heir to the Kingdom, who by God's grace shall be a man of great might, through whom loss and dishonour, punishment and great shame, full of confusion and woe, shall befall your King'...

A Portent Of Death

In 1239 George Akropolites was a young courtier in attendance at the Byzantine palace in Nicaea, the city in Asia Minor from which the exiled Byzantine Emperor, John Doukas, planned the reconquest of Constantinople. His wife, Empress Irene, was a very educated person, interested in philosophy and science, two subjects that George had studied a little.

And when there was an eclipse, the sun travelling through the sign of Cancer at around midday, she [Empress Irene] asked me the cause of the eclipse. Now I couldn't give her a very precise answer because I had only just begun to cling to the secrets of philosophy as a young student of the wise teacher Blemmydes, but I had learned just enough so that it was reasonable for me to tell her the following:

I said that the cause of the darkening was due to the moon passing in front of the sun so that the sun appeared to lose its light; but it was not really a removal of the sun's heat and light but rather the effect of the moon when all of it enters into the shadow of the earth, for the moon takes its light from the sun.

I People praying below a sun figure. *Jacobus Omne Bonum*. English, 1360-80.

II Signalling St Cuthbert's death to Lindisfarne. From the *Life of St Cuthbert*, English 1100-99.

As the discussion went on for a very long time, and the doctor Nikolaos denied what I had said ⁄ he was a man who knew absolutely nothing of philosophy though he excelled in his own discipline and most especially in practical matters. He was also a great favourite of the empress and held the honour of court physician ⁄ now when he contradicted me and I was chattering away with many words, in the middle of this exchange, the empress called me a fool.

Then as if she had caused something inappropriate, she called to the emperor: 'I have done something unseemly when I called this boy a fool.' The emperor replied, 'It's not important, for he's only a lad.' For I was 21 years old so the term was not unsuitable. But the empress said in response: 'It's not right for anyone who brings forth philosophical words in this way to be addressed thus by us.' I have spoken of this exchange in order to show how greatly the empress loved learning and honoured those who were knowledgeable. Then she died... and I believe that the eclipse of the sun prefigured her death.

1 The battle of Gog and Magog that took place near Jerusalem. Gog is identified with the Antichrist in the commentary written in the margins of the Alba Bible, Maqueda, Spain 1422-30.

Crusading in the West

Pope Urban II's letter to the Counts of Besalú, Empuřias, Roussillon and Cerdaña, written between January 1096 and July 1099, points out that it is as worthy to fight against the Muslims in Spain as to go off to the East.

You know what a great defence it would be for Christ's people and what a terrible blow it would be to the Saracens if, by the goodness of God, the position of that famous city [of Tarragona in Spain] were restored. If the knights of other provinces have decided with one mind to go to the aid of the Asian Church and to liberate their brothers from the tyranny of the Saracens, so ought you with one mind and with our encouragement to work with greater endurance to help a church so near you to resist the invasions of the Saracens. No one must doubt that if he dies on this expedition for the love of God and his brothers his sins will surely be forgiven and he will gain a share of eternal life through the most compassionate mercy of our God. So if any of you has made up his mind to go to Asia, it is here instead that he try to fulfil his vow, because it is no virtue to rescue Christians from the Saracens in one place, only to expose them to the tyranny and oppression of the Saracens in another.

11 The Surrender of Antioch to the Saracens, the Greeks hand over the keys of the city in 632. *Livre des Merveilles*, France, *c.* 1405.

119

Crusading in the East

Part of a letter written from Antioch in October 1098 by Bruno, a citizen of Lucca who went on the First Crusade. It is addressed to all faithful Christians.

When we who were voyaging by sea had come to Antioch, the army, which had gathered together from everywhere by land, had already surrounded the city in siege, though not very well... Our princes decided to erect a fortress at the western gate of the city. This fortress, a very short ballista-shot away [from the city], is now called by the name of the Blessed Mary. There, on that same day, in an attack of the Turks, in which they killed 2,055 of our men, we killed 800 of the enemy. From the third day, moreover, when the fortress had been erected, until the

The War of Gath. Alba Bible, Maqueda, Spain, 1422-30.

third day before the Nones of June, our men endured many hardships, and, weakened by hunger and the sword, they toiled there at great cost. However, on this day the city was captured in the following manner: Four brothers, noble men of Antioch, on the second day of June promise to surrender the city to Bohemund, Robert Curthose, and Robert, Count of Flanders. These, however, with the common assent of all our princes, at nightfall conduct the whole army to the wall of the city, without the knowledge of the Turks. And in the morning, when the citizens of Antioch open the gates to receive the three named princes alone, according to promise, all of our men suddenly rush in together. There is the greatest clamour: our men obtain all the fortified places, except the very high citadel; the Turks, ╱ these they kill, those they hurl to destruction over the precipice.

Hunting

In his poem on the sparrowhawk, 'The Tale of the Alerion', Guillaume de Machaut makes a brilliant comparison between a hunting bird and a lady. Here, having trapped a particularly beautiful bird, he begins to train it to hunt.

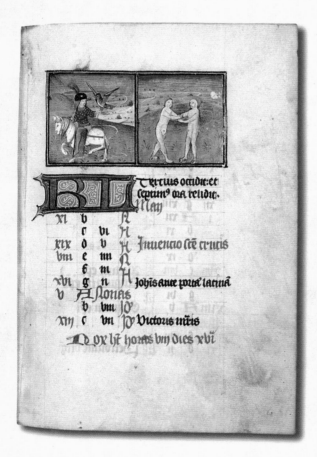

In any case, I heard a click
and knew that she was in the trap ‑
the noble, worthy Sparrowhawk.
Then I got up and went towards her,
and thus addressed the sparrowhawk:
'Dear friend, for you I've laboured long.
Though I've remained awake and toiled
already many nights for you,
henceforth I'll spend more sleepless nights,
for from this day my pain begins,
but that is pain that brings me joy
to my enjoyment and delight:
thus I can bear the pain with ease.'
    ... Then I took apart the structure
that was put together there,
and in the trap I carried off
the sparrowhawk, which gave me joy
until I came to my retreat
rejoicing, and, when I was there
began to train her joyously.
First I set to work to make
the hawk accustomed to my touch.
When I'd done this without a hitch,
and I could hold her on my fist,
I could see by her behaviour,
by her plumage and her manner,
she would be easy to instruct,
for she learned all things easily.

Then I took thought of how I should
provide for all that she would need,
so that at once I then arranged
that she should be provided for,
Then quickly I procured for her
lunes and creances of leather.
Then I abandoned every trace
of melancholy for her sake:
no other creature mattered now,

I The sign of Gemini and a hunting
scene from a fifteenth‑century astrological
manuscript written in Italy.

or any other enterprise,
not past or present, or to come...
   So I possessed entirely
the sparrowhawk I cherished so:
I valued her that much and more.
Valued? Why? It was quite right
for from the loving point of view,
it's clear from what I've told of her
that she was good in every way.
Above all, she was noble, true,
and possessed of every grace
expected of a sparrowhawk
that holds to its nobility,
in plumage elegant and sleek,
in manner gay and beautiful;
I've never seen a sparrowhawk
more noble or more well behaved,
more joyful or less difficult,
or one with less presumptuousness:
but always all the courtesy
one might find in a sparrowhawk ⁄
all these things one could find in her,
so that I kept her joyfully.
   Now I have adorned this well
when to the lady I've compared
the sparrowhawk, which always did
unfailingly what pleased me best.
My pleasure, I may well believe,
was nurtured by sufficiency,
for she was never once inclined
to do what might have displeased me:
at least, it so appeared to me,
she carried off my heart so well.
And she was then the more inclined
to let me hold and carry her.
Indeed such gracious services
were an easy burden for me.

II 'And he seized the knife to slaughter it and the bird opened its beak and sang.'

III 'Image of the hawk hanging.' Copied from *Fables of the Ancients*, a fifteenth-century book of moralistic tales.

Disruption of Trade

A letter from Isaac Nisaburi, a Jewish trader in Alexandria, to a colleague in Fustat reports on bad sailing conditions, which brought the silk trade to a standstill in September 1118.

At the arrival of the Spanish ship, all business stopped, no one sold and no one bought. After some days, small quantities were sold at the price of 21–2 (dinars) per ten (pounds).

When, however, all the ships tarried in coming, the merchants were eager to buy, but those who had silk kept it. Today it is thirty-three days that only one ship has arrived and only one ship has sailed. Now there is much confusion and worry about the ships. For today it is twenty-three days from the Feast of the Cross and not a single ship has arrived from the Maghreb, nor has any news come from there. The winds are adverse, neither east nor west. On this very day they paid for coarse silk 23 dinars. No one sold or will sell until it is known what it will be. So please, do not move with the silk except in the event that trustworthy unravellers are available to whom you might give a small reel to unravel, good only for the countryside...

Kindest regards to you and all the friends.
And may your well-being wax indefinitely.

Top: Two spice merchants riding on laden camels next to the sea. Ships in the distance transport spices to the East. Pliny the Elder, *Historia Naturalis.*

The Old Nun

In the ninth century, Theodora, a wealthy young widow entered a convent in Thessaloniki. She became a most devout nun and took care of the elderly mother superior in her final illness.

When the blessed Theodora was in her fifty-sixth year... the mother superior [Anna], while walking in the courtyard without anyone to guide her, slipped and fell; and the head of her thighbone was dislocated from the right socket located at the sacral bone beneath her lower back. And from that time on she was unable to move and was confined to bed. After she had been bedridden for four years, her mind also became confused because of her extreme old age...

Then one could see the blessed Theodora ministering almost alone to Anna's every need, carrying her and frequently shifting her position, bringing her food with her own hands and taking her to the bath, and in general taking total care of her, even though Anna reviled and hit her...

When the blessed Theodora was in her sixty-eighth year, the great confessor Anna, who from childhood had donned the holy monastic habit and by the grace of God had lived a blameless life, found repose in the death that is owed to the righteous. The entire span of her life was reputedly 120 years.

II Top:'Image of the Man of God speaking in the manner for which he is praised. And the author listens because he has inclined his ear to him.' From *Fables of the Ancients,* a book of Hebrew morality tales copied here from a fifteenth-century miscellany.

III Below: A biblical illustration of the story of Jephthah's daughter, depicted in the garb of a medieval nun.

herre gepoten hat durch die
hant moysi zu den kindern
israhels in den veldungen
moab ouf dem iordan gegé
iericho · zcetera· Die hat das
buch das do genant ist das
buch der zcal ein ende· Dor
nach hebt sich an das buch
Deutronomnus das do ist
also gesprochen das buch
der anderweidunge der· e·

as sint die wort die do geredt
hat moyses zu allem israel
vber den iordan in den velden
der wustenunge gegen dé
roten mer (tzwischen vnd
tophel vnd laban vnd ase
roth) do etwas vil goldes ist
eilftag reise von oreb durch
den wek des pergis seir vntz
bis zu cades barne in dem

virtzigisten iare in dem eilften
manden an dem ersten tage
des menedis· Moyses redte
zu den kindern israhels alles
das im vnser herre hette gep
ten so das her in das sagte·
Dornach do her geslug den k
kving seon der amorren der
do wonte zu esebon· Vnd og
den kving basan der do won
te zu aseroth vnd zu edrai in
der erden moab· Vnd moyses
hub an zu berichten die e·
vnd zu sprechen· Vnser her
re got hat zu vns geredt zu
oreb sprechende· Genvgen
sol euch das ir ouf dem per
ge seit gewesen· kvmet vnd
widerkeret zu den pergen
der amorren vnd zu andn
steten des veldis· die in na
hen sint· Vnd zu den nidern
steten gegen mittem tage
Vnd bei dem vber des meres
die erden der chananeer vnd
des libanischen pergis vntz
bis zu dem grosen wasser eu
fraten· Secht sprach her euch
hab ich sie gegeben· Czihet
ein vnd besitzet die erde vber
die gesworn hat vnser herre
ewern vetern abraham ysa
ac vnd iacob so das her in
die gebe vnd irem samen noch
in· Vnd ich sagte euch in den
selben tzeiten· Ich mag nicht

A Miraculous Cure of Depression

The gold statue reliquary of St Foy at Conques in France attracted pilgrims from far and wide. This story is dated by the mention of Abbot Girbert to c. 1000.

In Auvergne there was a brave warrior named Bernard... After he returned from a journey to Rome, Bernard suffered a serious physical illness. Then, when he was just beginning to regain his strength, he was denuded of every lock of hair from his head, just as the leafy-tressed forests are deprived of all the beauty of their foliage by the Ides of September. He was so ashamed of his baldness, which seemed ugly to him, that he abandoned all his martial activities and stopped going to the places frequented by the noblemen who were his peers... he began to be troubled by so much depression, which we call weakness of mind, that he thought death more desirable than life.

One night while Bernard was resting quietly beneath his bedcovers and turning over many things silently in his mind, a deep sleep crept in and dissolved all his cares. While he was in this deep sleep... behold! the glorious martyr Foy came to him, and... she immediately burst forth with these commands: 'Do not delay to go confidently to the monastery at Conques. When you have arrived, make known to Abbot Girbert in my name that in my memory he should celebrate the divine mystery before the shrine of my body, while you stand on his left side until the reading of the holy Gospel has been completed. After the offertory, when the abbot has washed his hands, collect that water. He should moisten your head, and after that you must go over to the right side of the altar.'

Bernard awakened at daybreak, leapt up from his bed, and informed his mother about the night's vision in some detail... When she had gathered provisions for the journey, she and her son travelled to the monastery. There they told Abbot Girbert about the vision point by point, but he, as is usually the case with spiritually advanced persons, immediately protested that he was not worthy of being involved in such a business. His resistance was finally overcome by their urgent pleas and he devoutly carried out everything he had been directed to do. The following night while Bernard was keeping vigil in holy prayers before the sacred virgin's mortal remains, his scalp seemed to swell with little hairs, like the head of a newborn boy. And as he was returning to his home in the morning, his head began to grow so rosy red in colour that people thought the whole top of his head was stained with fresh blood. After he got home, Bernard shaved off all that hair with a razor. New hair appeared, thicker than before; he was clothed in tresses, and through the holy martyr's intercession he was found worthy of recovering the lost glory of his hair after being bald so long.

1 Bath maids washing hair from the Wenceslas Bible. Bohemian, 1390-1400.

Pleasure Gardens

The sixth-century historian, Procopius, recorded the achievements of the Emperor Justinian (527–65), including his monuments and public building works. Here he describes the pleasure gardens outside the Byzantine capital.

As one sails from the Propontis up toward the eastern side of the city, there is on the left a public bath. This is called Arcadianae, and it is an ornament to Constantinople, large as the city is. There this Emperor [Justinian] built a court which lies outside the city, and it is always open to those who tarry there for promenades and to those who anchor there as they are sailing by. This is flooded with light when the sun rises, and when it passes on toward the west it is pleasantly shaded. And the unruffled sea flows quietly about this court, encircling it with its stream, coming from the Pontus like a river, so that those who are promenading can actually converse with those who are sailing by. For the sea preserves its depth even though it reaches up to the very foundations of the court and so is navigable there for ships, and by reason of the deep calm which prevails it brings together those on land and those on the sea so that they can converse with each other. Such, then, is the side of the court which borders on the sea, adorned by the view over it, and breathed upon by the gentle breezes which come from it. Columns and marbles of surpassing beauty cover the whole of it, both the pavement and the parts above. And from these gleams an intensely brilliant white light as the rays of the sun are flashed back almost undimmed. Nay more, it is adorned with great numbers of statues, some of bronze, some of polished stone, a sight worthy of a long description. There also the Empress Theodora [wife of Justinian] stands upon a column, which the city in gratitude for the court dedicated to her. The statue is indeed beautiful, but still inferior to the beauty of the empress; for to express her loveliness in words or to portray it in a statue would be, for a mere human being, altogether impossible. The column is purple, and it clearly declares even before one sees the statue that it bears an Empress.

I Psalm 106 from the Anglo-Saxon copy of the Utrecht Psalter, early eleventh-century

II Opposite page: The first bible of Charles the Bald known as the Vivian Bible.
The scene shows a number of monks led by Vivian presenting the bible to the Emperor. Tours, France, *c.* 846.

Relics

In his account of Bishop Arculf's pilgrimage to the Holy Land in the seventh century, Adamnan, Abbot of Iona, preserved the story of how Caliph Muawiya (661–80) adjudicated rival claims on the shroud, now known as the Turin Shroud.

The king of the Saracens... said: 'Give into my hand the sacred cloth that you have.' They obeyed... took it forth from its reliquary, and laid it in his lap. The king took it with great reverence, and bade a pyre be prepared in the court before all the people. When it was burning with great intensity, he got up, went right up to the pyre,

and said in a loud voice to the dissident parties: 'Now let Christ the saviour of the world... judge by the flame of the fire between you who contend for this cloth, that we may know on which of these two contending bands he will deign to bestow such a gift.' And so saying he cast the Lord's sacred shroud into the flames. But the fire was completely unable to touch it. Whole and unimpaired it rose from the pyre, and began to flutter on high like a bird with outstretched wings gazing down from above on the two factions of the people... For a space of some minutes it fluttered about in the empty air, then gradually coming down it swerved by God's guidance towards the Christian party, who meantime kept beseeching Christ the judge, and it settled in their midst. Lifting their hands to heaven they give thanks to God with great rejoicing, and falling on their knees they receive with great honour this venerable gift sent down to them from heaven. They render hymns of praise to Christ its donor, and wrapping it in another cloth deposit it in a reliquary in the church. One day our brother Arculf saw it raised up from its reliquary, and in the crowded church kissed it himself amongst the multitude of people who were kissing it. It measures about eight feet in length.

I Personifications of Night and Dawn flank the prophet Isaiah. Constantinople, mid tenth-century.

II St John. Soissons Gospels, Court School of Charlemagne. Early ninth-century.

Relics of the Saints

On the route to Compostela, pilgrims were recommended by a twelfth-century guide book to visit the tombs of the saints at Arles.

First of all, those who go to Santiago by way of Saint-Gilles must visit in Arles the remains of the Blessed Trophimus the confessor... His feast is celebrated on December 29.

In like manner, one must visit too the remains of the Blessed Caesarius, bishop and martyr, who established in the same city the monastic rule and whose feast is celebrated on November 1.

In like manner, in the cemetery of the said city, the assistance of the Blessed Honoratus, bishop, should be invoked, whose solemn feast is celebrated on January 16, and in whose venerable and magnificent basilica the remains of the most illustrious martyr, the Blessed Genesius, are resting. There is... a village next to Arles called Trinquetaille where there is a certain magnificent and very high marble column... It is to this column, as it is told, that the perfidious populace tied the Blessed Genesius before beheading him. Even today it appears reddish from his rosy blood. No sooner had he been beheaded, than the saint himself, taking the head into his hands, cast it into the Rhone. As to his body, it was carried by the river as far as the basilica of the Blessed Honoratus where it honourably rests. The head, on the other hand, floating down the Rhone to the sea, led by an angel, reached Cartagena, a Spanish city, where now it splendidly rests and performs many a miracle. His feast is celebrated on August 25.

Subsequently, one should visit the cemetery next to the city of Arles, in a place called Alyscamps, and intercede there, as is customary, for the deceased with prayers, psalms, and alms. Its length and width are one mile each. In no cemetery anywhere, except in this one, can one find so many and so large marble tombs set upon the ground. They are of various workmanship and bear antique engravings...

A monk takes a cart bearing St Edmund's relics across the bridge to the Monastery of Bury St Edmunds. From *The Life of St Edmund*, c. 1130.

Old Age

After many years of living separately and chastely, Margery Kempe was summoned to look after her elderly husband. This English text written in about 1443 graphically illustrates many familiar problems of old age.

It happened one time that the husband of the said creature [Margery] ⁄ a man of great age, over sixty years old ⁄ would have come down from his chamber bare⁄foot and bare⁄legged, and he slithered, or else missed his footing, and fell to the ground from the stairs, with his head twisted underneath him, seriously broken and bruised, so much that he had five lined plugs in the wounds in his head for many days while his head was healing...

And, as God willed, it was known to some of his neighbours how he had fallen down the stairs, perhaps through the din and the rushing of his falling. And so they came in to him and found him lying with his head twisted under himself, half alive, all streaked with blood, and never likely to have spoken with priest nor clerk, except through high grace and miracle.

Then... his wife [Margery] was sent for, and so she came to him. Then he was taken up and his head was sewn, and was ill for a long time after, so that people thought he would die... She took her husband home with her and looked after him for years afterwards, as long as he lived. She had very much trouble with him, for in his last days he turned childish and lacked reason, so that he could not go to a stool to relieve himself, or else he would not, but like a child discharged his excrement into his lined clothes as he sat there by the fire or at the table, wherever it was, he would spare no place. And therefore her labour was all the greater, in washing and wringing, and so were her expenses for keeping a fire going. All this hindered her a very great deal from her contemplation, so that many times she would have disliked her work, except that she thought to herself how she in her young days had had very many delectable thoughts, physical lust, and inordinate love for his body. And therefore she was glad to be punished by means of the same body, and took it much the more easily, and served him and helped him, she thought, as she would have done Christ himself.

I 'Image of the miser trapped in his denial and his wife gives him balm to drink as his soul leaves him.'

II Right: The Caladrius bird was known for its power to foretell whether a sick person would live or die. If it turned away, the person was doomed but if it inclined its face towards him, he would recover.

castor. venator. castor.

Tem est animal quod dicitur castor nimis mansue
tum. Nam in medicina testiculi ei tene pdesse dicun
tur contra diuersas inualitudines. Phisiologus ex
posuit naturam eius dicens. Qui cum inuestigat
fuerit a uenatore. respiciens post se q uidens uenato

Inquisition

In central France in the thirteenth century, the inquisitor, Stephen of Bourbon, discovered practices connected with the cult of St Guinefort, the Holy Greyhound, which he considered most reprehensible.

I should speak of offensive superstitions, some of which are offensive to God, others to our fellow men. Offensive to God are those which honour demons or other creatures as if they were divine; it is what idolatry does, and it is what the wretched women who cast lots do, who seek salvation by worshipping elder trees or making offerings to them scorning churches and holy relics, they take their children to these elder trees, or to ant hills, or to other things in order that a cure may be effected.

This recently happened in the diocese of Lyons where, when I preached against the reading of oracles, and was hearing confession, numerous women confessed that they had taken their children to Saint Guinefort. As I thought that this was some holy person, I continued with my enquiry and finally learned that this was actually a greyhound...

Above all, it was women with sick or weak children who took them to this place [where the greyhound had been buried]... We went to this place, we called together all the people on the estate, and we preached against everything that had been said. We had the dog disinterred, and the sacred wood cut down and burnt, along with the remains of the dog. And I had an edict passed by the lords of the estate, warning that anyone going henceforth to that place for any such reason would be liable to have his possessions seized and then sold.

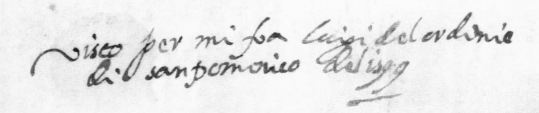

I Top: The beaver was hunted mercilessly for its testicles which were said to contain medicinal properties. Accustomed to their fate, they would bite off their own testicles, leaving them for their hunters so that their lives at least might be spared.

II 'Seen by me, Luigi of the Order of San Domenico, 1599'. The censor's comments on a Hebrew manuscript. Barcelona, *c.* 1348.

The Black Death

The Black Death provided Boccaccio with the setting for his Decameron - *one hundred stories told by seven ladies and three young men, who in 1348 sought refuge from the plague outside Florence.*

Thus, for the countless multitude of men and women who fell sick, there remained no support except the charity of their friends (and these were few) or the greed of servants, who worked for inflated salaries without regard to the service they performed and who, in spite of this, were few and far between... Out of sheer necessity, there arose among those who remained alive customs which were contrary to the established practices of the time.

With the fury of the pestilence increasing... there were many who passed away without having even a single witness present, and very few were granted the piteous laments and bitter tears of their relatives... Very few were the dead whose bodies were accompanied to the church by more than ten or twelve of their neighbours, and these dead bodies were not even carried on the shoulders of honoured and reputable citizens but rather by gravediggers from the lower classes that were called *becchini*. Working for pay, they would pick up the bier and hurry it off, not to the church the dead

I In the city of Jerusalem, men carry coffins and prepare others.

man had chosen before his death but, in most cases, to the church closest by, accompanied by four or six churchmen with just a few candles, and often none at all. With the help of these *becchini*, the churchmen would place the body as fast as they could in whatever unoccupied grave they could find without going to the trouble of saying long or solemn burial services.

The city was full of corpses... things had reached such a point that the people who died were cared for as we care for goats today... So many corpses would arrive in front of a church every day and at every hour that the amount of holy ground for burials was certainly insufficient for the ancient custom of giving each body its individual place; when all the graves were full, huge trenches were dug in all of the cemeteries of the churches and into them the new arrivals were dumped by the hundreds; and they were packed in there with dirt, one on top of another, like a ship's cargo, until the trench was filled...

More than one hundred thousand human beings are believed to have lost their lives for certain inside the walls of the city of Florence, whereas before the deadly plague, one would not even have estimated there were actually that many people dwelling in the city.

II Top: The valley of dry bones. The image reflects Ezekiel's vision of the resurrection of the dead after the coming of the Messiah.

III Saul consults the witch at En-dor. Alba Bible, Maqueda, 1422-30.

Coping with Plague

The Black Death, which ravaged Europe in the years 1347–51, caused a major demographic disaster, reducing the population by perhaps as much as a quarter. Among those who survived it, Tommaso del Garbo developed hygienic practice that remained standard for centuries.

Notaries, confessors, relations and doctors who visit the plague victims on entering their houses should open the windows so that the air is renewed [i.e. the corrupt air], and wash their hands with vinegar and rose water and also their faces, especially around their mouth and nostrils. It is also a good idea before entering the room to place in your mouth several cloves and eat two slices of bread soaked in the best wine and then drink the rest of the wine. Then when leaving the room you should douse yourself and your pulses with vinegar and rose water and touch your nose frequently with a sponge soaked in vinegar. Take care not to stay too close to the patient.

The Epitaph of Harald

In the second half of the tenth century, this rune epitaph was carved on the Jelling stone, which was erected at Jutland, Denmark.

King Harald ordered this monument to be made in memory of Gorm, his father, and in memory of Thyre, his mother. This was the Harald who conquered the whole of Denmark and Norway, and made the Danes Christian.

I Top left: Monks with plague being blessed by a priest. Jacobus Omne Bonum, English, 1360-80 .

II Left: The death of a king. Latin Bestiary, 1260-80.

III Top: A Viking warship. Anglo-Saxon view of the Viking raids, 1025-50.

IV A regal burial. Alba Bible, Maqueda, Spain, 1422-30.

A Miraculous Icon

In the late thirteenth century, Manuel Philes wrote a series of epigrams associated with the shrine of the Virgin of the Source in Constantinople. The female patron who commissioned this one is otherwise unknown.

On behalf of Kasiane Raoulaina to an icon of the Mother of God

O you who delivered Eve from her intense suffering
  And do sympathetically watch over my birth pangs
(For God [was born] of you without the natural pain of childbirth)
  Accept this thank-offering, holy Virgin,
  You, through whom my infant child who all but died
Lives and breathes beyond [all] hope.
  For you are life and the source of miracles,
    Washing away the mud of sin.
  Maria Kasiane, the daughter of Raoul,
  of the lineage of the Komnenoi,
    Has spoken these words to you in gratitude.

Birth

In his Memoirs, *Guibert of Nogent (c. 1064–c. 1125) describes his own birth.*

As she approached the end of her pregnancy my mother had been in the most intense pain throughout the season of Lent. How often she reproached me in later years for those pangs of childbirth when she saw me straying and following the slippery downhill path! Finally Holy Saturday, the solemn vigil of Easter, dawned. My mother was wracked with continuous pain. As the hour of delivery approached, the pains increased, but they were presumed to lead to a natural delivery. Then I turned around in her womb, with my head upward. My father, his friends, members of the family, all feared for both our lives. The child, they thought, was hastening the mother's death; and the offspring's exit from the world at the very moment he was being denied an entrance into it added to their sense of pity... The family held an urgent meeting. They rushed to the altar of the Mother of God, to the one who was, and ever will be, the only Virgin to give birth, they made the following vow and left it as an offering at our lady's altar: if the child were male, it would be consecrated a cleric in God's service and hers; if the child were of the lesser sex, it would be given over to a corresponding religious vocation.

At that moment a frail little thing came forth, looking almost like an aborted foetus, except that it was born at term. It looked like a most miserable being, and the only reason for rejoicing was that the mother had been saved. This tiny human being that had just seen the light was so lamentably frail that it looked like the corpse of a stillborn baby... On the same day, as I was brought to the baptismal font... a woman kept rolling me over from one hand to the other and saying: 'Do you think this little creature's going to live? I guess Mother Nature never quite finished this one. She gave him an outline more than a body.'

... If it is obvious and irrefutable that one's merits cannot precede the day of one's birth, they can, nevertheless, precede the day of one's death; but if one's life is spent without doing good, then I think it makes no difference whether the day of one's birth, or death, was glorious or not.

I Right: Eve gives birth to Cain, her hand raised to her head in an expression of pain that denotes how he was born tainted with original sin. The tree of knowledge is seen here with two types of leaves. The serpent points his red tongue of blame at Eve. Adam in the earlier scenes has blond hair but later it becomes red to signify his sin. The scenes are linked by the River of Paradise.

II Opposite page: The legendary Dame Trotula of Salerno was attributed authorship of the best known work on obstetrics in the Middle Ages. She was hailed as 'an empress among midwives' and is seen here holding an orb.

Cohitus

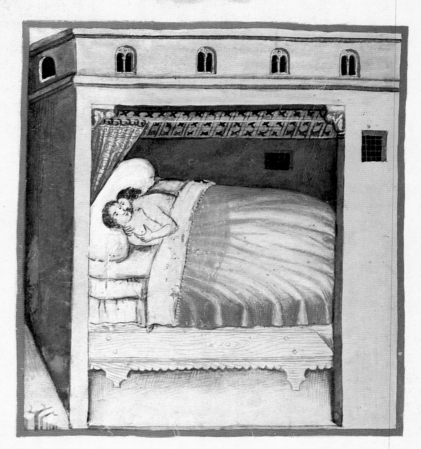

Restriction of Prostitution

In this regulation of 1393, the City of London tried to restrict the activity of female prostitutes, identified by their hoods of striped cloth.

... and whereas many and divers affrays, broils, and dissensions, have arisen in times past, and many men have been slain and murdered, by reason of the frequent resort of, and consorting with, common harlots, at taverns, brewhouses of hucksters [peddlers] and other places of ill-fame, within the said city, and the suburbs thereof; and more especially through Flemish women, who profess and follow such shameful and dolorous life: ⁄ we do by our command forbid, on behalf of our Lord the King, and the Mayor and Alderman [sic] of the City of London, that any such women shall go about or lodge in the said city, or in the suburbs thereof, by night or by day; but they are to keep themselves to the places thereunto assigned, that is to say, the Stews [bathhouses] on the other side of the Thames, and Cokkeslane; on pain of losing and forfeiting the upper garments that she shall be wearing, together with her hood, every time any one of them shall be found doing to the contrary of this proclamation.

I The Marriage Bed. *Theatrum Sanitatis.* Italian, *c.* 1400.

II Opposite page: The Bath House. Valerius Maximus, *Des faits des Romains*, French, fifteenth-century.

Reform of Prostitution

The Byzantine Emperor, Michael IV (1031–41), was a great philanthropist. His contemporary, the historian Michael Psellus, describes how 'he devised a plan for the salvation of lost souls'.

Scattered all over the city was a vast multitude of harlots, and without attempting to turn them away from their trade by argument ⁻ that class of woman is deaf anyway to all advice that would save them ⁻ without even trying to curb their activities by force, lest he earn the reputation of violence, he built in the Queen of Cities a place of refuge to house them, an edifice of enormous size and very great beauty. Then, in the stentorian notes of the public herald he issued a proclamation: all women who trafficked in their beauty, provided they were willing to renounce their trade and live in luxury, were to find sanctuary in their building: they were to change their own clothes for the habit of nuns, and all fear of poverty would be banished from their lives for ever... Thereupon a great swarm of prostitutes descended upon this refuge, relying on the emperor's edict, and changed both their garments and their manner of life, a youthful band enrolled in the service of God, as soldiers of virtue.

Phebus montant auecques ses
cheuaulx tenoit humble teste du
ciel que vesta eut ce cest adiuc
que Le soulcil estoit en signe

Ballade

Dante (1265–1321)
began his lyrical work,
New Life, *aged twenty-seven,*
two years after the death
of Beatrice, who inspired it.

Ballade, I want you to seek out Love,
and with him go before my lady...
With sweet melody, when you are with him,
begin these words,
after you have asked for mercy:
'My lady, he who sends me to you,
when it pleases you, desires
that if he had an excuse you may hear it from me...
Tell her: 'My lady, his heart has attended
with such steadfast faith
that in your service he has been moulded by every thought:
from the first he has been yours, and never has he strayed.'
... Through the grace of my sweet melody
remain here with her,
and of your servant speak what you will;
and if through your prayer she forgives him,
have her fair countenance announce to him peace.
My gentle ballade, when it pleases you,
go forth at that moment when you may receive honour.

I Top: 'Sing to the Lord.' Below the staves are the
words, 'There is none like thee among the gods' written
in Hebrew. From a thirteenth-century book of Psalms.

II Opposite page: Emily making a garland. Giovanni
Boccaccio, French, *c.* 1470.

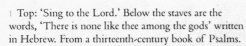

An Accusation of Rape

Froissart records a case of alleged rape, which occurred in 1386 when Sir Jean de Carrouges left his wife in charge of their castle and a local squire, Jacques Le Gris, took advantage of his absence. The account opens with a description of the squire.

[He] was a man of humble birth who had risen in the world, favoured by fortune as many people are. But when they are right on top and think themselves secure, fortune flings them back into the mire and they end up lower than they began...

It happened that Sir Jean de Carrouges made plans to go on an expedition overseas ⁄ a thing he had always been fond of doing ⁄ to help him in his advancement. He bid his wife who was young, beautiful, good, sensible and modest in her behaviour a loving goodbye, as knights do when they leave for distant lands...

It then happened ⁄ and this was the whole point at issue ⁄ that, through a strange, perverse temptation, the devil entered the body of Jacques Le Gris... His thoughts became fixed upon Sir Jean de Carrouges' wife, who he knew was living almost alone with her servants in the castle of Argenteuil. So he left Alençon one day on a good horse and spurred swiftly forward until he reached the castle. The servants welcomed him in, because he and their master both served the same lord and were companions⁄in⁄arms. In the same way, the lady, not suspecting anything wrong, gave him a friendly reception, led him to her room and showed him a number of her things. Bent on his evil design, Jacques asked the lady to take him to see the keep, saying that that was partly the object of his visit. The lady agreed without question and the two of them went to it alone...

No sooner had they entered the keep than Jacques le Gris shut the door behind him. The lady paid little attention to it, thinking that the wind had blown it shut... And when they were alone there together, Jacques Le Gris, ensnared by the wiles of the Enemy, put his arms round her and said: 'Lady, I swear to you that I love you better than my life, but I must have my will of you.'

The lady was astounded and tried to cry out, but the squire stuffed a little glove which he carried into her mouth to silence her, gripped her tight for he was a strong man and pushed her down to the floor. He raped her, having his desire of her against her will. When this was done, he said: 'Lady, if you ever mention what has happened, you will be dishonoured. Say nothing and I will keep quiet too for your honour's sake.' The lady, weeping bitterly, replied: 'Ah, you wicked, treacherous man, I will keep quiet but not for as long as you will need me to.'

She then opened the door of the room in the keep and came down, followed by the squire...

The young wife shut herself in her room and there gave way to bitter lamentations... She revealed nothing to any of her servants, feeling sure that if she did so she was more likely to incur blame than credit. But she fixed firmly in her memory the day and the time when Jacques Le Gris had come to the castle.

I Above: 'The Little Nun Who Left Her Convent and Walked Off Into the Century.' The young nun escapes from her convent but takes the veil again thirty years later after seeing the Virgin in a dream. By the renowned and prolific early fourteenth-century artist, Jean Pucelle.

II Opposite page: 'The Lover Contemplates his Lady.' From *Le Remède de Fortune c.* 1350, one of the outstanding works of the fourteenth-century.

Trial by Combat

When Sir Jean de Carrouges was told by his wife that she had been raped by the squire Jacques Le Gris, he believed her innocence and tried to obtain justice on her behalf, while Le Gris denied everything. The fourteenth-century chronicler, Froissart, records the outcome of their dispute.

The legal proceedings went on for more than a year and a half... After much deliberation and argument the court pronounced that, since the lady of Carrouges could not prove anything against Jacques Le Gris, the matter should be settled by a duel to the death...

The day of the combat arrived at about the beginning of the year counted as 1387 according to the custom of Rome. The lists were prepared in St Catherine's Square, behind the Temple. The King of France was there with his uncles and vast crowds of people came to watch... Before the knight entered the lists, he went over to his wife, who was sitting clothed in black in a carriage draped entirely in black also, and said to her: 'Lady, on your evidence I am about to hazard my life in combat with Jacques le Gris. You know if my cause is just and true.' 'My lord,' said the lady, 'it is so. You can fight confidently. The cause is just.' 'In God's hand be it then,' said the knight. He kissed his wife, pressed her hand, then made the sign of the cross and entered the lists...

When the two champions had taken the oath, as is usual before such combats, they were placed opposite each other and told to say why they had come together. They then mounted their

1 A mock joust between children riding deer. The lances are rendered inoffensive by two small white pinwheels.

horses and sat them very prettily, for both were skilled in arms. The first part of the combat was a joust, in which neither of them was injured. They then dismounted and continued on foot, both fighting very courageously. The first to suffer was Sir Jean de Carrouges, who was wounded in the thigh, to the great alarm of his supporters, but he fought on so stoutly that he felled his opponent, and, thrusting his sword into his body, killed him on the spot. He turned and asked whether he had done his duty and was told that he had. Jacques Le Gris' body was delivered to the executioner of Paris, who dragged it to Mountfaucon and hanged it there.

Then Sir Jean de Carrouges went up to the King and kneeled before him. The King made him rise and presented him with a thousand francs, making him also a member of his chamber with a pension of two hundred francs a year for life. After thanking the King and the great nobles, the knight went to his wife and kissed her, then they went together to the Cathedral of Notre-Dame to make their thank-offerings before returning to their house.

11 The jousts of St Ingelvert. Froissart's *Chronicle,* French, late fifteenth century.

Swimming

In the ninth century, the Frankish court poet and historian, Einhard, wrote a biography of the Emperor Charlemagne. He captures much of the ruler's character through descriptions of his activities.

The Emperor was strong and well built... He spent much of his time on horseback and out hunting, which came naturally to him, for it would be difficult to find another race on earth who could equal the Franks in this activity. He took delight in steam-baths at the thermal springs, and loved to exercise himself in the water whenever he could. He was an extremely strong swimmer and in this sport no one could surpass him. It was for this reason that he built his palace at Aachen and remained continuously in residence there during the last years of his life and indeed until the moment of his death. He would invite not only his sons to bathe with him, but his nobles and friends as well, and occasionally even a crowd of his attendants and bodyguards, so that sometimes a hundred men or more would be in the water together.

1 Pharoah in a suit of golden armour seen crossing the Red Sea in pursuit of the Israelites. The illuminator follows the biblical text: 'You split the sea before them; they passed through the sea on dry land, but You threw their pursuers into the depths, like a stone into the raging waters.'

11 Scenes from a fourteenth-century treatise on bathing and the taking of thermal baths.

Rape

In 1405, Christine de Pizan wrote her most famous prose work, The Book of the City of Ladies, *in which Reason, Justice and Rectitude help her to construct a city peopled by distinguished women. Here she consults Rectitude about the argument*

made by men that many women want to be raped, even when they protest verbally.

[Rectitude] answered, 'Rest assured, dear friend, chaste ladies who live honestly take absolutely no pleasure in being raped. Indeed, rape is the greatest possible sorrow for them...

The story of the noble queen of the Galatians, the wife of King Orgiagon, is appropriate to this subject. When the Romans were making their great conquests in foreign lands, they captured this king of the Galatians in battle, and his wife along with him. While they were in the Roman camp, the noble queen, who was quite beautiful, simple, chaste and virtuous, greatly pleased one of the officers of the Roman army, who was holding the king and queen prisoner. He entreated her and coaxed her with fine presents, but after he saw that pleading would not work, he violently raped her. The lady

suffered terrible sorrow over this outrage and could not stop thinking of a way to avenge herself, biding her time until she saw her chance. When the ransom was brought to deliver her husband and herself, the lady said that the money should be turned over in her presence to the officer who was holding them. She told him to weigh the gold to have a better count, so that he would not be deceived. When she saw that he intended to weigh the ransom and that none of his men would be there, the lady, who had a knife, stabbed him in the neck and killed him. She took his head and without difficulty brought it to her husband and told him the entire story and how she had taken vengeance...

It was the same when a city in Lombardy was once captured by its enemies who killed the lord. The beautiful daughters of this lord, thinking that their enemies were going to rape them, found a strange remedy, for which they deserve much praise: they took raw chicken meat and placed it between their breasts. This meat quickly rotted because of the heat so that when the enemies approached them and smelled the odour, they immediately left, saying, 'God, how these Lombards stink!' But this stink made them quite fragrant indeed.

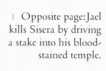
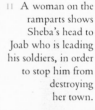

I Opposite page: Jael kills Sisera by driving a stake into his blood-stained temple.

II A woman on the ramparts shows Sheba's head to Joab who is leading his soldiers, in order to stop him from destroying her town.

Winter

From the chronicle written in the early ninth century by Theophanes, a Byzantine monk.

In the same year [762], starting in early October, there was very bitter cold, not only in our land, but even more so to the east, the north, and the west, so that on the north coast of the Pontos to a distance of 100 miles the [Black] sea froze from the cold to a depth of thirty cubits... All this ice was snowed upon and grew by another twenty cubits, so that the sea became indistinguishable from land: upon this ice wild men and tame animals could walk from the direction of Chazaria, Bulgaria and other adjoining countries. In the month of February of the same second indiction this ice was, by God's command, split up into many different mountain-like sections, which were carried down... the Straits... and reached the City and filled the whole coast... Of this I was myself an eyewitness for I climbed on one of those icebergs and played on it together with some thirty boys of the same age... One of the icebergs struck the jetty of the Acropolis and crushed it. Another huge one struck the wall and shook it greatly so that the houses on the inside partook of the quake. It then broke into three pieces and ringed the City from the Mangana to the Bosphoros, rising in height above the walls.

I Above: A fishing scene from an eleventh-century Greek manuscript.

II Opposite page: Foetal positions. Physicians had puzzled over how to depict the foetus in the womb for several centuries, in particular over the question of twins emerging simultaneously. English, fifteenth-century manuscript.

An Orphaned Child

This tenth-century account records the capture of three Greek monks and a boy living in southern Italy by Arab pirates from Africa, and their successful ransom.

In the district of Calabria there is a monastery inhabited by pious and virtuous monks, one of whom found a child for sale. He purchased the child and raised him with care. He also taught him how to read and write in the hope of tonsuring him and clothing him with the monastic habit. One day, three of the monks decided to go down to the sea to fish and as they went along, they took the child with them. When they came to the sea, some Saracens from Africa were there with their ship and seized them. When the abbot and fathers of the monastery learned of this, they suffered no small grief, especially the monk who was master to the boy. [He then offered to go and ransom the captives.]

As he was walking through the market place [in Africa], his child came face-to-face with him. Taking and embracing him, the monk asked him with tears in his eyes: 'Oh child! What has become of you?' The child replied: 'Worthy father, a man who is an enemy of God purchased me. He abuses me every day, coercing me to become a Muslim. But my trust is in God and in your holy prayers that I will not do that, even if I have to die.'

... [The monk works various miracles and is summoned to the African ruler.] The Prince of Believers said: 'Since it has been made known to us that you are a servant of God, we will surrender the three monks and the youth to you free of charge. This we do so that you will remember us too in your prayers to God.'

Piracy

The journeys of the Polo brothers to the Great Khan of China between 1260 and 1295 involved Marco's return through India.

You must know that from Malabar, and from the neighbouring province called Gujarat, more than 100 ships cruise out every year as corsairs, seizing other ships and robbing the merchants. For they are pirates on a big scale. I assure you that they bring their wives and little children with them. They spend the whole summer on a cruise and work havoc among the merchants...

Gujarat likewise is a great kingdom. The people are idolaters and have a king and a language of their own and pay tribute to none. The country lies towards the west. Here the Pole Star is still more clearly visible, with an apparent altitude of six cubits. In this kingdom are the most arrant corsairs in the world. Let me tell you one of their nasty tricks. You must know that, when they capture merchants, they make them drink tamarind and sea-water, so that they pass or vomit up all the contents of their stomachs. Then the corsairs collect all that they have cast up and rummage through it to see if it contains any pearls or precious stones. For the corsairs say that when the merchants are captured they swallow their pearls and other gems to prevent their discovery. That is why they do not scruple to treat them to this drink.

I Opposite top:
The island of Sumatra.

II Opposite bottom: How the soldiers of the Great Khan were unable to land in Java. *Livre des Merveilles* an anthology of Marco Polo's travels between 1271 and 1295, written around 1405 and presented to Jean, Duc de Berry in 1413.

Dangerous Games

The Book of Chivalry, written by a French knight in the mid-fourteenth century, set standards for all forms of courtly behaviour.

All young men who desire to attain... an honourable status... should not concern themselves too much with nor devote too much attention to any game where greed might overcome them, such as the game of dice, for it is no longer a game when it is engaged in through greed for gain. And what usually happens is that when one thinks one will win another's money, one loses one's own, and there are many who lose three hundred, five hundred, a thousand *livres*, and more of their money...

There is also a game called real tennis at which many people lose and have lost some of their chattels and their inheritance; and while playing such games, one would not want to see nor meet any men of good standing for whom it would be necessary to leave the game and speak to them and keep them company. One should leave playing dice for money to rakes, bawds, and tavern rogues...

The situation is the same for real tennis; women have greatly suffered over this, for ball games used to be women's pastime and pleasure. Yet it should be apparent that the finest games and pastimes that people who seek such honour should never tire of engaging in would be in the pastimes of jousting, conversation, dancing, and singing in the company of ladies and damsels as honourably as is possible and fitting, while maintaining in word and deed and in all places their honour and status.

Top: The valiant knight saves the damsel in distress from the jaws of the green dragon.

Left: Scipio and Laelius play chess while Scaevola plays pelota.

Music

In the twelfth-century Anglo-Norman epic, The Romance of Horn, *musical expertise is highly praised.*

In those days everyone knew how to play the harp well: the higher the rank, the greater the knowledge of the art. It was now Gudmod's turn to entertain them with it... He did not want to refuse them... Then he took the harp, for he wanted to tune it. Lord, whoever then watched his knowledgeable handling of it, how he touched the strings and made them vibrate sometimes causing them to sing and at other times join in harmonies, would have been reminded of the harmony of heaven! Of all the men there, this one caused most wonder. When he had played his notes, he began to raise the pitch and to make the strings give out completely different notes. Everyone was astonished at his skilful handling of it. And when he had done this, he began to sing the lay of Baltof... loud and clearly, just like the Bretons, who are versed in such performances. Next he made the harp strings play exactly the same melody as he had just sung. He performed the whole lay for them and did not want to omit any of it. And Lord, how his audience then had occasion to love him!

Above: A scene from the Barcelona Haggadah. Written before 1248, the manuscript is an important early source for musicologists as it contains twenty-eight different musical instruments.

Courtship

When Horn, disguised as the less high-born Gudmod, arrived at court, he attracted the attention of not only the king's sons, who took him hunting, but also their sister Lenburc. The Romance of Horn *records their courtship over a game of chess.*

One day as they returned from their sport in the forest, the king's sons had the idea that they would like to go and divert themselves in Lenburc's rooms: they would drink good wine, spiced and unspiced, with her, play chess and listen to the harp because those were the things they enjoyed most... The two brothers went to their sister's chambers. The elder brother took his chess-player with him who played very well – that was his entire occupation – and his strong knight, the best he had, and the younger took Gudmod, who was no boaster...

She called to a boy to fetch the chessmen and sat down with the expert player at the chessboard... The knight who was outplayed was very vexed...

Then on all sides they begged Gudmod to play and Lenburc greatly desired it above all the rest, so much did she long for them to be close enough together that he could be touched on hand or foot... They sat down and set out their chessmen and she who had checkmated the other man moved first.

Now they played the game in such a way that not a word was spoken suggesting discourtesy, but whatever was said expressed good manners. They played four games skilfully, one after the other, without her winning a fig's worth in any of the them. Nevertheless it seemed as if it did not grieve her, because she loved him so much she did not envy him. But if anyone else had done it, she would have been very cross, even had it been the king, who had so tenderly brought her up. Then Gudmod rose and Lenburc begged him to play one more game, for the love of his sweetheart. And Gudmod, laughing, gently admonished her not to entreat or say another word about it to him.

A lover presenting his songs to his lady from the Manasse Codex.

A Game of Chess

In The Ruodlieb, *an eleventh-century epic romance, the eponymous hero reports on his mission to a foreign kingdom, where the ruler negotiated over a game of chess.*

The king, asking for a table, ordered that a chair be brought for him and ordered me to sit down on the bench opposite him to play with him. I declined firmly, saying, 'It is fearful and lamentable to play against a king.' But when I saw that I dared not withstand him, I determined to play, hoping to be beaten by him. I said: 'Poor me! How can being beaten by the king hurt me? But, my Lord, I am afraid that you will soon be angry with me, if fortune is pleased to give the victory to me.' The king smiled and said as if in jest: 'My dear fellow, there is no need for you to have any fears in this matter. I shall not be roused to anger if I never win, but I want you to play with me as intently as you can; you see, I want to learn the moves you make of which I am ignorant.' At once the king and I began to play eagerly, and, may thanks be to her [Fortune], the victory fell to me three times; many of his nobles were utterly astounded at this. He laid a wager against me, but wanted me to wager nothing against him, and he gave me what he had put down, because he didn't have a pea left... I said: 'I am not in the habit of winning anything by playing games.' They (the nobles) replied: 'While you live amongst us, you live as we do! When you get back home, then you can live as you like.' I refused what they held out to me for a time, and then took them. Fortune gave me presents as well as praise...

I Chessplayers. Shirvan, 1468.

Normans

In September 1066 William of Normandy invaded England and defeated the Anglo-Saxon King Harold. The Anglo-Saxon Chronicle *preserves several accounts, including this one which reveals a particularly English point of view.*

Then Count William came from Normandy to Pevensey on Michaelmas eve, and as soon as they were able to move on they built a castle at Hastings. King Harold was informed of this and he assembled a large army and came against him at the hoary apple-tree. And William came against him by surprise before his army was drawn up in battle array... There King Harold was killed... and the French remained masters of the field... Count William went back to Hastings, and waited there to see whether submission would be made to him. But when he understood that no one meant to come to him, he went inland with all his army that was left to him and that came to him afterwards from overseas, and ravaged all the region that he overran until he reached Berkhamsted. There he was met by Archbishop Aldred and Edgar and Edwin and Morcar, and all the chief men from London. And they submitted out of necessity after most damage had been done... And they gave hostages and swore oaths to him. And he promised them that he would be a gracious liege lord, and yet in the meantime they ravaged all that they overran. Then on Christmas Day, Archbishop Aldred consecrated him king at Westminster. And he promised Aldred on Christ's book and swore moreover... that he would rule all this people as well as the best of the kings before him if they would be loyal to him. All the same he laid taxes on people very severely, and then went in spring overseas to Normandy, and took with him Archbishop Stigand, Edgar and Edwin and Morcar and many other good men from England. And Bishop Odo and Earl William stayed behind and built castles far and wide throughout this country, and distressed the wretched folk and always after that it grew much worse. May the end be good when God wills!

A Race

In The Saga of Sigurd the Crusader, *King Sigurd's son Magnus makes a bet with Harald Gille, who claimed that 'men may be found in Ireland, that no horse in Norway can run past them'.*

Magnus answered: 'I will not go to Ireland; we two shall bet here, and not there.' Harald then went to sleep and would have no more talk with him. This happened in Oslo. Next morning after Mass, Magnus rode up in the street; he sent word to Harald to come there. And when he came he was clad in this way; he had on a shirt and breeches with straps, a short cape, an Irish hat on his head, and a spear shaft in his hand. Magnus set up a mark for the race. Harald said: 'You make the run too long.' Magnus straightway made it much longer and said that this was even then all too short. Many men were present. They then began the race and Harald always kept pace with the horse. And when they came to the end, Magnus said: 'You held to the saddle strap and the horse pulled you.' Magnus had a very fast horse from Gautland. They now ran the race again and Harald ran all the time in front of the horse. And when they came to the end of the race, Harald asked: 'Did I hold on to the saddle strap then?' Magnus said: 'You were first off.'

Then Magnus let his horse breathe a while, and when he was ready, he smote the horse with his spurs and straightway came at a gallop. Harald then stood still and Magnus looked round and shouted: 'Run now,' he said. Then Harald ran and at once came forth past the horse and much farther in front and so to the end of the race; he was so much to the fore that he lay down and sprang up and greeted Magnus when he came.

I Horses were regarded as being completely loyal beasts
and are depicted here fighting alongside their masters.
Bestiary Latin, *c.* 1255.

A Boar Hunt

Before keeping his appointment with the Green Knight, Sir Gawain stayed at an unknown castle and spent Christmas with an unidentified castellan. He was encouraged to sleep late while his host, who was in fact the Green Knight, went out hunting.

The cock having crowed and called only thrice,
The lord leaped from bed, and his liegemen too,
So that mass and a meal were meetly dealt with,
And by first light the folk to the forest were bound
For the chase. Proudly the hunt with horns
Soon drove through a desert place;
Uncoupled through the thorns,
The great hounds pressed apace.
By a quagmire they quickly scented quarry and gave tongue,
And the chief huntsman urged on the first hounds up,
Spurring them on with a splendid spate of words.
The hounds, hearing it, hurried there at once,
Fell on the trail furiously, forty together,
And made such echoing uproar, all howling at once,
That the rocky banks round about rang with the din.

Hunters inspirited them with
    sounds of speech and horn.
Then together in a group, across
    the ground they surged
At speed between a pool and a
    spiteful crag.
On a stony knoll by a steep cliff
    at the side of a bog,
Where rugged rocks had roughly
    tumbled down,
They careered on the quest, the
    cry following,
Then surrounded the crag and
    the rocky knoll as well,
Certain their prey skulked inside
    their ring,
For the baying of the bloodhounds
    meant the beast was there.
Then they beat upon the bushes
    and bade him come out,
And he swung out savagely
    aslant the line of men,
A baneful boar of unbelievable size,
A solitary long since sundered
    from the herd,

Being old and brawny, the biggest of them all,
And grim and ghastly when he grunted: great was the grief
When he thrust through the hounds, hurling three to earth,
And sped on scot-free, swift and unscathed.
They hallooed, yelled, 'Look out!' cried, 'Hey, we have him!'
And blew horns boldly, to bring the bloodhounds together...
Then men shoved forward, shaped to shoot at him,
Loosed arrows at him, hitting him often,
But the points, for all their power, could not pierce his flanks,
Nor would the barbs bite on his bristling brow...
But when the boar was battered by blows unceasing,
Goaded and driven demented, he dashed at the men,
Striking them savagely as he assailed them in rushes,

I Above: The temptation of Sir
Gawain by the wife of his opponent
from *Sir Gawain and the Green Knight*,
c. 1400, possibly the earliest illustrated
work of literature in English.

II Opposite page: November.
A hunting scene from a German
manuscript calendar. The enraged
boar is trapped in a snare in a winter
landscape.

165

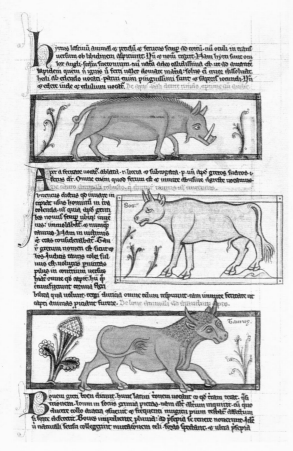

So that some lacking stomach stood back in fear.
But the lord on a lithe horse lunged after him,
Blew on his bugle like a bold knight in battle,
Rallied the hounds as he rode through the rank thickets,
Pursuing this savage boar till the sun set...
The castellan coursed across the country time and again,
Hunted his hapless boar as it hurtled over the hills...
But in time he became so tired he could tear away no more,
And with the speed he still possessed, he spurted to a hole
On a rise by a rock with a running stream beside.
He got the bank at his back, and began to abrade
    the ground,
The froth was foaming foully at his mouth,
And he whetted his white tusks; a weary time it was
For the bold men about, who were bound to harass him
From a distance, for none dared to draw near him...
Till the castellan came himself, encouraging his horse,
And saw the boar at bay with his band of men around.
He alighted in lively fashion, left his courser,
Drew and brandished his bright sword and boldly
    strode forward,
Striding at speed through the stream to where the savage
    beast was.
The wild thing was aware of the weapon and its wielder,
And so bridled with its bristles in a burst of fierce snorts
That all were anxious for the lord, lest he have the worst of it.
Straight away the savage brute sprang at the man,
And baron and boar were both in a heap
In the swirling water: the worst went to the beast,
For the man had marked him well at the moment of impact,
Had put the point precisely at the pit of his chest,
And drove it in to the hilt, so that the heart was shattered,
And the spent beast sank snarling and was swept downstream,
Teeth bare.
A hundred hounds and more
Attack and seize and tear;
Men tug him to the shore
And the dogs destroy him there.

III Top: Bestiary Latin, *c.* 1255.

Teaching

The following story records a situation well known to both teachers and pupils. It was written by Arcoid, canon of St Paul's, London, in the mid-twelfth century.

In the catholic community of St Paul's in London there was a certain scholar, Elwin by name, a man noted for his morality and learning...

One day he had expounded to one of his pupils, in the usual grammar-school fashion, a passage that the boy was to recite the following day, and he threatened him repeatedly with a severe flogging if he should not be able to recite it...

The boy, on the other hand, who was at that tender, undisciplined age, was seduced by his peers into playing games, and forgot both his teacher's warning and his own lessons. On the following day, when the time for the recitation was at hand... the boy could not think of any way of saving the situation... After much fretting and anguishing it occurred to [him] that he might avoid and escape punishment by fleeing or by praying to a special person... He quickly got up and fled away and came to the church in which rested the body of St Erkenwald, and there he prostrated himself at St Erkenwald's side. It has not been revealed to human understanding what the boy said as he prayed... we must believe, however, that his contrite, humbled heart was pleasing to God...

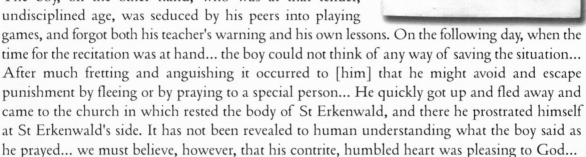

Well, the master... went into the school as usual and when he did not find the boy there, realizing that he had run away, he acted on intuition and came straight to the place where the boy was lying in humble prayer to the saint... The teacher dragged him out of the church and made him stand in the school to suffer his angry judgement... It pleased the schoolmaster... to hear the boy recite to him; he intended that as often as he found him making an error in his lesson he would give him two stripes with the rod...

But by the prayers and merits of Erkenwald, himself a wonderful teacher, wisdom was suddenly with the boy... not only did he repeat, without stumbling and without assistance, what the master had assigned, but also, to the latter's amazement, he recited at length and completely from memory what the teacher had been about to give him for the next assignment! Then indeed the teacher came to his senses... and forgave the boy.

I Above: A medieval hand ball game.

II Top: An elementary grammar for use in St Paul's School, London, published in 1515.

EXPLICIT LIB QVI VOCAT ECLE
SIASTES INCIP LIB QVI APPEL
LATVR HEBRAICE SYRA SYRI
LATINE CANTICA CANTICORVM

VOX ECCLESIE DESIDE
RANTIS ADVENTV XPI.

sunt ubera tua uino · fraglantia unguentis
optimis · Oleum effusum nomen tuum. ideo

Dance

In the fifteenth century, Guglielmo Ebreo of Pesaro wrote a treatise on The Art of Dancing.

Whoever wishes diligently to pursue the science and art of dancing with a joyful spirit and a sincere and well-disposed mind must first understand, with resolute heart, reflecting mind, and with consideration, what dance is in general and its true definition; which is none other than an outward act which accords with the measured melody of any voice or instrument. This act is composed of and bound to six rules or principal elements which are the following: Measure, Memory, Partitioning the Ground, Air, Manner, and Body Movement. These six elements must be minutely and perfectly grasped and kept well in mind, for if one of these is lacking in any way, the art [of the dance] would not be truly perfect... They are the foundation, the means, and the true introduction to the complete and perfect art of the dance.

Rules for women

It behoves the young and virtuous woman... to behave and conduct herself with far more discretion and modesty than the man. She therefore should fully understand and observe perfectly the aforesaid elements, rules, and exercises... The movement of her body should be humble and meek, and her carriage dignified and stately; her step should be light and her gestures shapely. Nor should her gaze be haughty or roaming (peering here and there as many do), but she should for the most part keep her eyes modestly on the ground; not, however, as some do who sink their head on their breast. Rather, she should carry it upright, aligned with the body, as nature itself - as it were - teaches us. And when she moves she should be nimble, light, and restrained... Then at the end of the dance, when released by the man, she should, turning her sweet gaze on him alone, make a courteous and tender bow in answer to his...

On Dancing In Long Attire

Note that someone dancing in a long garment should dance with solemnity and in a different fashion... All his gestures and movements should be grave and as refined as his attire requires, and of an apt fashion, because the *turca* or long robe that he is wearing would not work with too much moving here and there... since a short garment requires dancing a little more vigorously...

On Dancing With A Cape

Note further that another sort of dancing is required when wearing a short cape as opposed to a *turca* or even a [short?] garment. And the reason is, the cape catches the wind, so that as you do a jump or a turn, the cape swings about. And with certain gestures and movements, and with certain rhythms, you need to hold your cape by an edge, and with [other] rhythms you have to hold both edges, which is a lordly thing to see when done in time. And if this is not done when the rhythms require it, it is a sign of little skill.

Opposite page: King Solomon and the Queen of Sheba.
From The Song of Songs, Winchester Bible.

Dance Song

An anonymous Provençal dance song of the twelfth century about a loveless marriage: Coindeta sui, si cum n'ai greu cossire.

I'll tell you why I'm someone else's lover:
(I'm lovely but miserable)
I'm fresh and young, I've a dainty body,
(I'm lovely but miserable)
and I ought to have a husband who can make me glad,
someone I can play and laugh with.
(I'm lovely but miserable
because of a husband I don't want or desire).

God knows I'm not the least in love
with him.
(I'm lovely but miserable)
I've little wish to make love with him.
(I'm lovely but miserable)
I'm filled with shame to look at him.
I wish that death would do him in.
(I'm lovely but miserable
because of a husband I don't want
or desire).

1 Male and female bathers exchange glances in a historiated letter which forms the first word of a chapter on bathing. From *Li livres dou santé*, by Aldobrandino da Siena.

But let me say one thing:
(I'm lovely but miserable)
this friend of mine makes it up to me in love,
(I'm lovely but miserable)
I indulge in fondest, sweetest hopes;
I cry and sigh when I don't see or gaze at him.
(I'm lovely but miserable
because of a husband I don't want or desire).

And let me say another thing:
(I'm lovely but miserable)
since my friend has loved me a long time,
(I'm lovely but miserable)
I'll indulge in love
and fondest hopes for the one I crave.

(I'm lovely but miserable
because of a husband I don't want or desire).

I've made a pretty dance song to this tune,
(I'm lovely but miserable)
and I ask everyone to sing it, far and wide.
(I'm lovely but miserable)
And let all learned ladies sing it too,
about my friend whom I love and long for.
(I'm lovely but miserable
because of a husband I don't want or desire).

II Above left: Psalm 33 from a thirteenth century Psalter: 'Praise the Lord with the lyre…Sing to him a new song, play skilfully on the strings…'

III Above right: From a fourteenth century thunder-chart, illustrated for the benefit of semi-literate people. In this instance the image suggests there should be 'Concord among the people.'

Entertainments

During the marriage feast of the Infanta Doña Blanca and the Infante Don Enrique in 1440, elaborate constructions were built in order that the guests could overlook the jousting as well as a pond and a copse during the four-day fiesta.

The knights and gentlemen danced at the palace; there were also mummers, running of bulls, and jousts... On the fourth day, the Count had an immense room built in a large fenced meadow behind his palace. In this artificial hall, a very high stage was built, requiring twenty steps to ascend to the top. It was covered with grass to look like a natural mound. There sat the Queen, the princess and the countess of Haro on rich scarlet brocade, as befitted such great ladies.

On the side of the meadow, there was a list for a joust with twenty knights and gentlemen. On the other side there was a pond which had been specially stocked for the feast with large trout and barbel. As the fish were caught, they were brought to the princess. In another part of the meadow, there was a beautiful copse of trees, which the Count had ordered to be stocked with bears, boars, and deer. The wood was surrounded by almost fifty huntsmen with 'gentle' mastiffs, greyhounds and hounds in such a manner that no animal was able to escape. Unleashing the dogs, the huntsmen pursued and killed the beasts and brought them to the princess. And it seemed a very strange thing that in a house so many different sports could be carried out at the same time...

After the joust, the hunt and the fishing had been concluded, the dance began lasting almost all day... The Count generously distributed money to the trumpeters and minstrels from two large bags of coins...

That way the feast ended and all went to sleep the few hours of the night that were left.

I Opposite page: The opening page of Book IV of Virgil's *Aeneid*. Naples *c.* 1470-1500.

The Pleasures of Music

In his fifteenth-century treatise on dancing, Guglielmo Ebreo of Pesaro reflects on the 'sublime and lofty art of music', which he reckons to be not the least important of the seven liberal arts.

In some ways Music suits and befits human nature more than any other [art] inasmuch as, through the four principal and concordant voices of which it is formed and composed (corresponding to our four principal humours), it offers, as we listen, singular comfort to all our senses, as if it were our souls' most natural food. Nor does it seem that there is anyone in the world so uncouth and barbarous as not to be moved to utmost pleasure by the sweet song and the pleasant sound of a well-tuned instrument. Thus is it truly written of renowned Orpheus that he played his sweet-sounding *cithara* with such grace as to soothe not only the spirits of men, but wild Pluto and the infernal deities, as well as brutish animals, ferocious lions, and other savage beasts. The great sweetness [of music] also transmuted the very nature of rocks and hills into a more kindly one; as in the tale of Amphion of yore who, according to the poets, with the fair sound of his *cithara*, made the stones descend from the high hills and arrange themselves miraculously into the building of the high walls of the city of Thebes. And I could similarly describe many others who, through the sweetness and virtue of this delightful and most pleasurable science, wrought extraordinary changes and marvellous motions in the world.

I Three young, richly clothed couples move elegantly to the music played by two lutenists.

II Opposite page: Torch-dance at a feast; bowling hoops. From a Flemish calendar of the early sixteenth century.

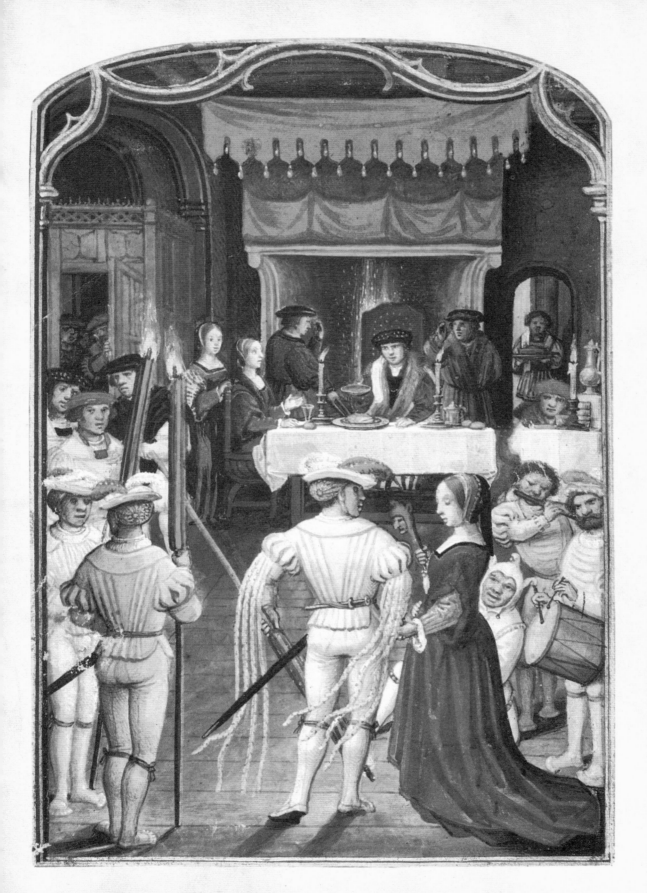

Prayer to the Virgin

St Anselm (1033–1109) served as Abbot of Bec and Archbishop of Canterbury in the period of Gregorian reform. He also wrote numerous works, including prayers.

Mary, holy Mary,
among the holy ones the most holy after God.
Mother with virginity to be wondered at,
Virgin with fertility to be cherished,
you bore the Son of the most High,
and brought forth the Saviour of the
lost human race.
Lady, shining before all others with
such sanctity,
pre-eminent with such dignity,
it is very sure that you are not least in
power and in honour.
Life-bearer, mother of salvation,
shrine of goodness and mercy,
I long to come before you in
my misery,
sick with the sickness of vice,
in pain from the wounds of crimes,
putrid with the ulcers of sin,
However near I am to death, I reach
out to you,
and I long to ask that by your
powerful merits
and your loving prayers,
you will deign to heal me.

Good Lady,
a huge dullness is between you and me,
so that I am scarcely aware of the extent of my sickness.
I am so filthy and stinking
that I am afraid you will turn your merciful face from me.
So I look to you to convert me,
but I am held back by despair,
and even my lips are shut against prayer...

I Above: Christ Enthroned. From a magnificent thirteenth-century choir book, Florence.

II Opposite page: The Genealogy of Christ.

 fuit est ties filius meus dilectus in te
bene complacuit mihi ⁘ ❊ ❊ ❊ ❊ ❊ ❊

Ipse ihserat incipiens quasi an
norum triginta ut putabatur filius

ioseph ❊ ❊ ❊ ❊ ❊

VI fuit ❊ heli ❊ ❊

VI fuit ❊ mathat ❊ ❊

VI fuit ❊ leui ❊

VI fuit ❊ melchi

VI fuit ❊ iaihie

VI fuit ❊ ioseph

VI fuit ❊ mathat hie

VI fuit ❊ amos

VI fuit ❊ nauum

VI fuit ❊ esli

VI fuit ❊ nagge

VI fuit ❊ enaath

Christmas

A fourteenth-century description of King Arthur's celebration of Christmas.

This king lay at Camelot one Christmastide
With many mighty lords, manly liegemen,
Members rightly reckoned of the Round Table,
In splendid celebration, seemly and carefree.
There tussling in tournament time and again
Jousted in jollity these gentle knights,
Then in court carnival sang catches and danced;
For fifteen days the feasting there was full in like measure
With all the meat and merry-making men could devise,
Gladly ringing glee, glorious to hear,
A noble din by day, dancing at night!
All was happiness in the height in halls
  and chambers
For lords and their ladies, delectable joy...

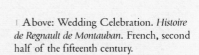

Mass sung and service ended, straight
  from the chapel
The King and his company came
  into hall.
Called on with cries from clergy
  and laity,
Noël was newly announced, named
  time and again.
Then lords and ladies leaped forth,
  largesse distributing,
Offered New Year gifts in high voices,
  handed them out,
Bustling and bantering about these offerings...
And all this merriment they made until meal time.
Then in progress to their places they passed after washing,
In authorised order, the high-ranking first;
With glorious Guinevere, gay in the midst,
On the princely platform with its precious hangings
Of splendid silk at the sides, a state over her
Of rich tapestry of Toulouse and Turkestan
Brilliantly embroidered with the best gems
Of warranted worth that wealth at any time
Could buy.

I Above: Wedding Celebration. *Histoire de Regnault de Montauban*. French, second half of the fifteenth century.

II Opposite page: Scenes from the Life of Christ. The De Lisle Psalter, English, fourteenth-century.

Snow

A harsh winter in 874 attracted the attention of the anonymous chronicler of the monastery of Fulda.

The winter was very hard and longer than usual; there were also great falls of snow from November 1 to the vernal equinox [March 21] without intermission, and these caused great difficulty to men wanting to go to the woods to collect fuel. Hence it came about that not only animals but also many men died of cold. The Rhine and the Main were frozen by the intense cold and for a long time would bear the weight of those who set foot on them.

I Opposite page: Hail beating the trees. Emilia, Italy, 1470-71.

II Above: It was said that the deeper a stallion placed his muzzle in water when he drank, the more virile he was likely to be. However, his virility would be impaired if his mane was cut. Bestiary in Latin, 1230-40.

The Virgin's Complaint

The Jewish poet, Immanuel of Rome (1261–1332), depicts the problems of a young girl with older sisters, who may never be able to raise the money for a dowry, and thus would never get married.

My breasts are firm and my hair is long, yet I still sit in nakedness and shame. My poverty has frightened away all the suitors, and I sit [as if] at the head of the table in a house of mourning.

How can my heart ever rejoice when all my silver is gone and I have no gold or bronze? How will I ever find a husband, when all I have are three older [impoverished] sisters and a groaning heart?

How can I tell, suitors, if my bones will be scorched [by desire] or if I will be able to strike a bargain with treacherous Time? My years are flying away, spreading their wings like locusts!

And what is more, the wise men sit and scheme together against me: 'She that dies a virgin is cut off; she will have no share in the world to come!'

Poverty

In the first half of the four-teenth century, this message was carved in runes on a wooden stick excavated in Bergen, Hordaland, Norway. It is a communication between two trading partners, Thorir and Havgrim, who rent business premises from a landlord in Bergen. Thorir here gives instructions to look after Sigrid and to conceal the bad news of his poverty, particularly from a man called Thorstein Long – for what reason we do not know.

Thorir the Fair sends God's and his own greetings, true fellowship and friendship to Havgrim, his partner. There is much I lack, partner. There is no beer, nor is there any fish. I want you to know this, and don't ask anything from me. Tell the landlord to come south to see how things are with us. Encourage him to do this, but demand nothing for my sake; and don't let Thorstein Long know about any of this. Send me some gloves. If Sigrid needs anything, then get it for her. Promise me that you will not rebuke me for my poor state.

Top: David and Bathsheba. David leans down from a flat roof and watches Bathsheba bathing, her long hair falling over her naked breasts.

11 Astronomers at the top of Mount Athos. From the travels of Sir John Mandeville, Bohemia, fifteenth century.

XP AVTEM
GENERAT
SIC ERAT CVM ESSET D
ESPONSATA MATEREIVS
MARIA IOSEPH ANTEQVA
CONVENIRENT INVENTA
EST INVTERO HABENS

The Will of Alfred

Before his death in 899, the Anglo-Saxon King Alfred revised his will and destroyed all copies of the previous one he had made.

... I, Alfred, king of the West Saxons, by the grace of God and with this witness, declare what I desire concerning my inheritance after my lifetime. First, I grant to Edward my elder son the land at Stratton... and Hartland... and I entreat the community at Cheddar to choose him on the terms which we have previously agreed...

And to my two sons 1,000 pounds, 500 pounds each; to my eldest daughter, to the middle one, to the youngest and to Ealhswith... 100 pounds each. And to each of my ealdormen 100 mancuses [a money of account worth 30 pennies], and to Æthelhelm, Æthelwold, and Osferth likewise. And to Ealdorman Æthelred a sword worth 100 mancuses. And to the men who serve me, to whom I have just now given money at Eastertide, 200 pounds are to be given and divided between them... And to the archbishop 100 mancuses, and to Bishop Esne and to Bishop Werferth and to the bishop of Sherbourne. Likewise, 200 pounds is to be distributed for my sake, for my father and the friends for whom he used to intercede and I intercede, fifty to the mass-priests throughout all my kingdom, fifty to the poor servants of God, fifty to the poor and destitute, fifty to the church in which I shall rest. I do not know for certain whether there is so much money, nor do I know whether there is more, though I suspect so. If there is more, it is to be shared among all those to whom I have bequeathed money...

My grandfather had bequeathed his land on the spear side and not on the spindle side. If, then, I have given to any one on the female side what he acquired, my kinsmen are to pay for it... because they are receiving my property, which I may give on the female side as well as on the male side, whichever I please.

And I pray in the name of God and of his saints that none of my kinsmen or heirs oppress any of the dependants among those whom I have supported; and the councilors of the West Saxons

I Above: *The Anglo-Saxon Chronicle* was the first history of England written in the vernacular and was commissioned by King Alfred during his reign, 871-99.

II Previous page: The portraits of the Evangelists, St Matthew and St John probably produced at Canterbury in the mid-eighth century. The script and ornament unite in a composition of astonishing virtuosity.

pronounced it right for me that I could leave them free or servile, whichever I should choose. But I desire for the love of God and for the needs of my soul that they be entitled to their freedom and their free choice. And in the name of the living God I command that no man should oppress them either with claims for money or with anything, in such a way that they cannot choose whatever lord they desire.

The Death of Guillaume Champlitte

The fourteenth-century Chronicle of Morea *records the conquest and occupation of southern Greece by western crusaders after 1204. Guillaume Champlitte, grandson of the first Prince of Morea, died in 1278.*

He drew up his will with great care... He commanded and ordered that after he had died, and not before a full year had passed, his bones alone were to be placed in a coffin in the church of St Jacob of Morea in Andravida, in this church which he had built and which he had given to the Temple, in the tomb he had built and in which lay his father; his brother to lie to the right of him, he to be on the left, and his father in between. He instructed and endowed four chaplains, whom all the Romans call *heireis* [priests], to continue without cease unto eons of eons to chant and celebrate masses everlastingly for their souls...

And when he arranged all these things... he surrendered his soul, and the angels took it and bore it to where all the righteous are found; commemorate him, all of you; he was a good prince. Behold the evil that befell, for which the small and great of Morea must grieve, for he did not leave a male, son of his body, to inherit the land which his father had won with such travail. But, on the contrary, he produced daughters and his labours went wasted; for it is never found established that a female child may inherit a lord's inheritance, for at the very beginning a curse was laid upon woman; and never in his life should a lord who had produced daughters as heirs rejoice...

I Above: St Alban's Psalter. The Entombment, *c.* 1119-23

II Right: Four scenes from the Gospels. Constantinople, eleventh century.

187

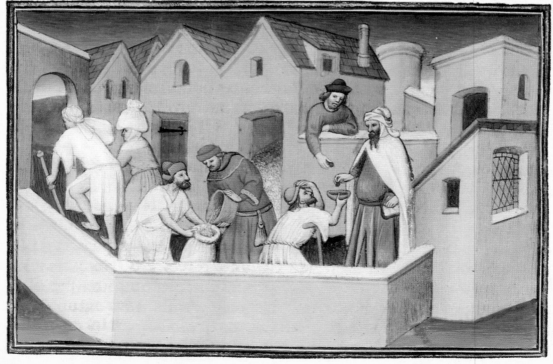

I Above: Distribution of wheat and alms by the Great Khan in times of famine. '*Livre des Merveilles*', a magnificent manuscript about Marco Polo's travels. France, *c.* 1405.

II Top: The annual birthday celebration of the Great Khan.

Riches

Sir John Mandeville's account of his travels to the Far East, probably written in 1355, proved immensely popular, despite the fact that it was mainly a pastiche of information from other accounts.

The land of Cathay is a great country, beautiful, rich, fertile, full of good merchandise. Every year merchants come there to get spices and other sorts of merchandise ⁄ they go there more frequently than they do elsewhere. You should understand that the merchants who come from Venice or Genoa or other places in Lombardy or the Greek Empire travel by land and sea for eleven or twelve months before they get to Cathay, the chief realm of the Great Khan...

The Emperor can spend as much as he wishes to, for he coins no money except from leather, or paper, or the bark of trees. When this money gets old, and the printing on it is defaced by heavy use, it is brought to the king's treasury and his treasurer gives new for old. This money is printed on both sides, like money is in other countries, and it is current throughout the Great Khan's lands. They make no money there of gold and silver, when it is

brought thither by different nationalities from other lands, but the Emperor has his palace adorned with it and makes useful things of it as he pleases. In his chamber on a pillar of gold is a ruby and a carbuncle, each a foot long; and this carbuncle lights all the chamber at night. He also has many precious stones and rubies in his chamber; but those two are the greatest and most precious of all.

III Top: 'Image of the diligent loyal one, with a great crown of gold and with a garment of fine linen and purple.'

IV Above: 'Image of the eagle and his guests eating.' *Fables of the Ancients*, from the Rothschild Miscellany, Italy, 1470-80.

Travel

In the years 1399–1402 Emperor Manuel II Palaiologos made a long tour of European capitals in search of military aid for the Byzantine Empire against the Turks. From London early in 1401, he wrote to his teacher and friend, Manuel Chrysoloras.

Now what is the reason for the present letter?... Most important is the ruler with whom we are now staying, the king of *Bretania* the Great [Henry IV, 1399–1413], of a second civilized world, you might say, who abounds in so many good qualities and is adorned with all sorts of virtues...

This ruler, then, is most illustrious because of his position, most illustrious too because of his intelligence; his might amazed everyone, and his understanding wins him friends; he extends his hand to all and in every way he places himself at the service of those who need help. And now, in accord with his nature, he had made himself a virtual haven for us in the midst of a twofold tempest, that of the season and that of fortune, and we have found refuge in the man himself and in his character. His conversation is quite charming he pleases us in every way; he honours us to the greatest extent and loves us no less. Although he has gone to extremes in all he had done for us, he seems almost to blush in the belief ‧ in this he is alone ‧ that he might have fallen considerably short of what he should have done. This is how magnanimous the man is... In the end he has given greater proof of his nobility by adding a crowning touch to our negotiations, worthy of his character and of the negotiations, themselves. For he is providing us with military assistance, with soldiers, archers, money and ships to transport the army where it is needed.

[Sadly, Manuel was to be disappointed in the amount of help forthcoming, but the Mongol defeat of the Turks in 1402 brought Byzantium some relief.]

I Above: 'Image of the judge and the eloquent ministers consulting and taking counsel'.

II Right: An encounter between an old king and a young black woman. From *Fables of the Ancients*, by Isaac Ibn Sahula, 1281, part of the Rothschild Miscellany, Italy 1479.

Vout le seigueur de aiblay kaan qui estoit seigueur des tartars
de tout le monde. et de toutes les pouinces vignes et regions
de ceste disine partie du siecle et entendu tont le fait des latis
si comme les .ij. fres lui auoient compte si lui plot moult.
Si pensa a soy mesmes denuoier les messages a lapostolle.
Si leur pria moult daler en celle messaguerie auec vn de ses

A Byzantine Emperor Abroad

Manuel II's visit to London in 1401 was commented on by many observers, including the chronicler, Adam of Usk.

This Emperor always walked with his men, dressed alike and in one colour, namely white, in long robes cut like tabards; he finding fault with the many fashions and distinctions in dress of the English, which he said indicated fickleness and changeable temper. No razor touched head or beard of his chaplains. These Greeks were most devout in their church services, which were joined in as well by soldiers as by priests, for they chanted them without distinction in their native tongue... I thought within myself, what a grievous thing it was that this great Christian prince from the farther east should perforce be driven by unbelievers to visit the distant lands of the west, to seek aid against them.

1 How the Great Khan sent his brothers with messages for the Pope. *Livre des Merveilles,* early fifteenth century.

Death

In the mid-eleventh century, the Byzantine historian, Michael Psellus, lost his daughter in an outbreak of smallpox. This is part of the oration he wrote for her funeral.

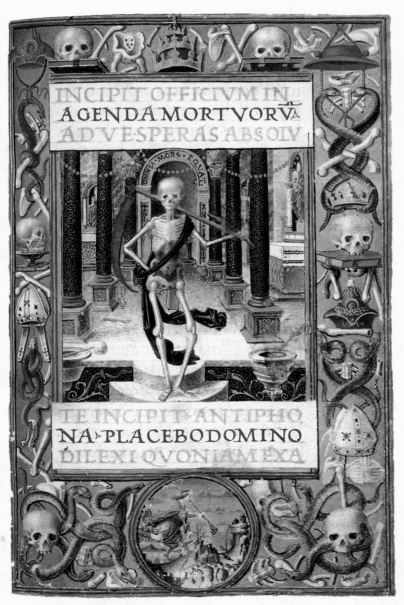

God let this maiden, so good, so modest and so beloved, be encircled by pestilential disease... It began by altering the entire structure of the body, and in the beginning filled it with fever. Then blisters appeared and spread like grapes all over the surface of the skin and having destroyed the harmony of her body left it horrible to see...

So she lay there crushed by innumerable, festering sores (in number and kinds one could hardly imagine). They were around the openings of her ears, around her nostrils, in her throat and even on the palate of her mouth, causing pain and difficulty in the ailing girl. But as the twentieth day dawned we had better hopes: for the sores dried up and began to fall from her body like flakes. But then suddenly what happened to her, who seemed like a wrecked ship that had just been towed to port? Violent fever came on, we know not from where or how, and it consumed the remaining flesh while she lay there as if embalmed. Yet she endured the unbelievable flames without complaint... She displayed fortitude like a diamond...

Above: Death, the 'Grim Reaper.' *Mirandola Hours.* Written in Padua or Venice, *c.* 1499.

When the maiden sensed that the end was near, as she was unable to speak or cry out, she motioned to her mother with senseless, inarticulate sounds. Then raising her hands a little, hands that had been destroyed by sores and were without skin or bones, she joined these to her mother's and gave what I thought was the last embrace. This gesture burned and tore the mother's heart and brought streams of tears to the eyes of all those present. For they were parents too and shared our woe...

But then the moment of death passed and the thirtieth day came and she lay there, voiceless and in a hurry to leave this world. The crowd of people around her were crying and striking their breasts in lamentation, and wished that they too could die along with the expiring girl. Then she gave up her spirit to the glowing angels standing by her side.

O my child, formerly so beautiful and now a frightful sight to see!... Go then on that good, eternal journey, and rest in those heavenly places. Shine in spirit among the Prudent Virgins. And reveal yourself in our dreams as you were prior to your illness, bringing solace to our hearts... You will thus bring joy to your parents; and they may recover a little from this heavy sorrow.

It has been shown that nothing is stronger than Nature; nor is there anything more calamitous than the loss of a child.

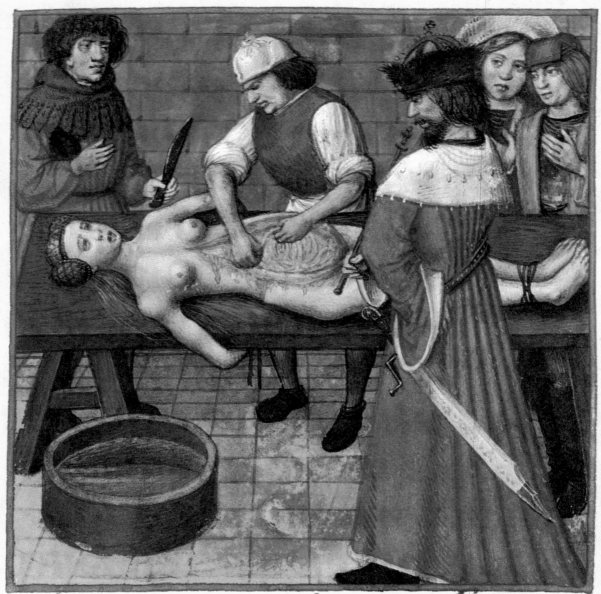

Et pour ce que beoir il wuloit
Le lieu ouquel conceu lauoit

Nero watches while his mother is dissected.
From the *Roman de la Rose*, Flemish, *c.* 1500.

Burial

The ceremony of burial of William of Trumpington, Abbot of St Alban's monastery on 27 February 1235.

The body was stripped and washed and, if he had not shaved the day before, his tonsure and beard would certainly have to be shaved. Then some, but by no means all, of the more senior and prudent monks and a single secular servant, namely the sacrist's assistant, who was to undertake the task of anatomist, were admitted, and the body was opened with an incision from the trachea to the lower part. Everything found in it was placed, sprinkled with salt, in a cask, which was reverently interred in the cemetery with blessings and psalms... The body was washed

and soaked inside with vinegar, a great deal of salt was sprinkled into it, and it was sewn up. This was done with care and prudence lest the body, which had to be kept for three or more days, should give off an offensive smell and occasion some unpleasantness to those handling it when it was buried. By this time, not without the admiration of many, the body was so clean and spruce, and the face so rubicund and unblemished, that to many it seemed pleasant and desirable to touch it with their hands and carry it on their

shoulders like some saint. And so you would see some of the brothers grieving, wringing their hands, weeping, lamenting, and gently and tenderly kissing his vivid face while embracing him with both hands; for he looked as if he was asleep, rather than dead...

The body was carried into the church, while a bell was solemnly peeled, and the convent followed it singing the customary psalms. There, in the sight of the entire convent and anyone else who was present, the abbot's seal was broken with a hammer on a stone step in front of the high altar, so that all the embossing, that is the image and the lettering, was effaced. From then on there was no lack of solemn and assiduous psalmody, by night and by day; and solemn mass [was celebrated] daily at the high altar as is the custom for a deceased brother, in albs at prime and in copes for those in the choir, with numerous candles lit. This continued till the day of his reverent obsequies... Meanwhile, a lengthy distribution of alms to the poor was made, while everyone groaned over the loss of such a great and good shepherd of souls and bodies.

1 Becket takes leave of Pope Alexander III fortified by his support. English, *c.* 1230-40 .

A Byzantine View of Crusaders

In 1204 the historian Niketas Choniates was inside the city of Constantinople when the western crusaders broke through the triple walls and thoroughly sacked the Byzantine capital. He gives here an eye-witness account of his family's escape.

There was a certain acquaintance of mine who shared my hearth with me, a Venetian by birth, who was deemed worthy of protection, and with him, his household and wife were preserved from physical harm. He proved to be helpful to us in those troubled times. Putting on his armour and transforming himself from merchant to soldier, he pretended to be a companion in arms and, speaking to them in their own barbaric tongue, claimed that he had occupied the dwelling first. Thus he beat off the despoilers to a man. But they continued to pour in in large numbers, and he despaired of opposing them, especially the French, who were not like the others in temperament or physique and boasted that the only thing they feared was heaven. As it was impossible for him to fall upon them, he enjoined us to depart...

We left a short time later, dragged away by the hand as though we had been allotted to him as captives of his spear, and downcast and ill-clad we were sent on our way... When our servants dispersed in all directions, inhumanly abandoning us, we were compelled to carry on our shoulders the children who could not yet walk and to hold in our arms a male infant at breast, and thus to make our way through the streets.

Having remained in the City for five days after her fall, we departed [17 April 1204]. The day was Saturday, and what had taken place was not, I believe, an event without meaning, a fortuitous circumstance or a coincidence, but the will of God. It was a stormy and wintry day... As we came to the Church of the Noble Martyr Mokios, a lecherous and unholy barbarian, like a wolf pursuing a lamb, snatched from our midst a fair-tressed maiden, the young daughter of a judge. Before this most piteous spectacle our entire company shouted out in alarm. The girl's father, afflicted by old age and sickness, stumbled, fell into a mud-hole, and lay on his side wailing and wallowing in the mire; turning to me in utter helplessness... he entreated that I do everything possible to free his daughter. I immediately turned back and set out after the abductor, following his tracks; in tears I cried out against the abduction, and with gestures of supplication I prevailed upon those passing troops who were not wholly ignorant of our language to come to my aid, and I even held on to some with my hand...

When we arrived at the lodgings of this lover of women, he sent the girl inside and stood at the gateway to repulse his opponents. Pointing my finger at him, I said, 'This is he to whose wrong-doing the light of day bears witness, and who disregards the commands of your wellborn chiefs... This man has flouted your injunctions before many witnesses and was not afraid to bray like a salacious ass at the sight of chaste maidens. Defend, therefore, those who are protected by your laws and who have been put in our charge'...

With such arguments, I aroused the sympathies of these men, and they insisted on the girl's release. At first, the barbarian showed contempt, as he was held captive by the two most tyrannical of passions, lust and wrath. When he saw, however, that the men were bristling with anger and proposed to hang him from a stake as an unjust and shame-less man... he yielded reluctantly and surrendered the girl. The father rejoiced at the sight of his daughter, shedding tears as libations to God for having saved her from this union without marriage crowns and bridal songs. Then he rose to his feet and continued on the way with us.

II Top: The fate of the adulterers. Maqueda, Spain 1422-30.

III Right: Phinehas the priest slays the fornicators by throwing a lance that penetrates their genitals. Alba Bible, Maqueda, Spain 1422-30.

Easter Regulations

As the holiest festival of the ecclesiastical calendar, the celebration of the Resurrection, which brought to an end the period of fasting associated with Lent, was also a feast. But churchmen were anxious that Christians should not enjoy too many additional pleasures, as the canon passed in 692 makes clear.

From the holy day of the Resurrection of Christ until New Sunday, the faithful are to frequent the holy Churches without ceasing during the entire week, with psalms and hymns and spiritual songs. Rejoicing in Christ and celebrating, listening to the reading of holy Scripture and delighting in the holy Mysteries; for thus shall we arise and be exalted together with Christ. In no wise, then, ought horse-races or public spectacles to be performed during the aforesaid days.

Calculating the Date of Easter

Conflicting methods of calculating the date of Easter were resolved at the Synod of Whitby, on the north-east coast of England in 664. Here the great historian and polymath, Bede (673–735), describes the consequences of adopting the Roman system.

Not long afterwards, those monks of Irish extraction who lived in Iona, together with the monasteries under their rule, were brought by the Lord's guidance to canonical usages in the matter of Easter... The monks of Iona accepted the catholic ways of life under the teaching of Egbert... In the year of our Lord 729, when Easter fell on 24 April, after he had celebrated a solemn mass in memory of the Lord's resurrection, he departed to be with the Lord on the same day. So he began the joyful celebration of the greatest of all festivals with the brothers whom he had converted to the grace of unity, and completed it, or rather continues the endless celebration of it, with the Lord and His apostles and the other citizens of heaven. It was a wonderful dispensation of the divine providence that the venerable man not only passed from this world to the Father on Easter Day, but also when Easter was being celebrated on a date on which it had never before been kept in those places.

Opposite page: The symbols for the Evangelists.
The Book of Kells, eighth to ninth century.

Easter in Jerusalem

Many pilgrims recorded their emotions at celebrating Easter in the shrine of the Holy Sepulchre in Jerusalem, which all Christians considered not only the holiest site but also the very centre (omphalos) of the entire world. Here is the account by a twelfth-century pilgrim, Theoderich.

It is customary in the church of the Holy Sepulchre, both in the church itself and in all the other churches in the city, at daybreak on the morning of Easter Eve, to put out the earthly lights, and to await the coming of light from heaven for the reception of which light one of the silver lamps, seven of which hang there, is prepared. Then all the clergy and people stand there waiting with great and anxious expectation, until God shall send his hand down from on high. Among other prayers, they often shout loudly and with tears, 'God help us!' and 'Holy Sepulchre!'

Meanwhile, the patriarch or some of the other bishops who have assembled to receive the holy fire, and also the rest of the clergy, bearing a cross in which a large piece of our Lord's cross is inserted, and with other relics of the saints, frequently visit the Holy Sepulchre to pray there; watching also whether God has sent his gracious light into the vessel prepared to receive it. The fire has the habit of appearing at certain hours and in certain places; for sometimes it appears about the first hour, sometimes about the third, the sixth, or the ninth, or even so late as the time of compline. Moreover, it comes sometimes to the sepulchre itself, sometimes to the Temple of the Lord, and sometimes to the Church of St John. However, on the day when our humble selves, with the other pilgrims, were awaiting the sacred fire, immediately after the ninth hour that sacred fire came, upon which, behold, with ringing of church bells, the

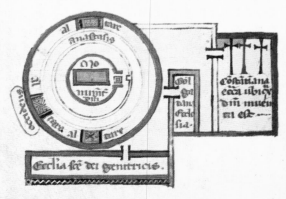

service of the Mass was said throughout the whole city, the baptismal and other services having been previously celebrated. As soon as the holy fire arrives, it is customary to present it to the Temple of the Lord before anyone, except the patriarch, has lighted his candle at it.

I Above: A woodcut illustration of Jerusalem. Part of a map by Bernhard von Breydenbach published in 1486 showing the Mediterranean at the foot and a westward view of Jerusalem. Many relevant landmarks are misplaced and Mount Sion and the Mount of Olives are shown close to each other whereas in fact they are on opposite ends of the city.

II Left: Plan of the Church of the Holy Sepulcre in Jerusalem from a fourteenth century manuscript describing Arculf's journey in 670.

Text Sources

19 'Spring'. From: T. Carmi (ed.), *The Penguin Book of Hebrew Verse* (Harmondsworth, Penguin, 1981), pp.420-1.

20 'Love'. From: Anon. 'Digenis Akrites' in David Ricks (ed. and tr.), *Byzantine Heroic Poetry* (Bristol Classical Press, 1990).

21 'Love Personified'. From: W. R. Paton (tr.), *The Greek Anthology* (Cambridge, MA, Harvard University Press/London, Heinemann, 1910, repr. 1980), vol.1, p.212.

22 'Mutual Love'. From: Peter Dronke, *Women Writers of the Middle Ages* (Cambridge University Press, 1984), p.94.

22 'Love's Radiance'. From: T. Carmi (ed.), *The Penguin Book of Hebrew Verse* (Harmondsworth, Penguin, 1981), p.343.

24 'Fortune-telling'. From: George Nedungatt and Michael Featherstone (eds.), *The Council in Trullo Revisited* (Rome, Pontificio Istituto Orientale, 1995), canon 61, pp.140-2.

25 'Whitsun'. From: 'The Romance of Horn' in Judith Weiss (tr.), *The Birth of Romance* (London, Everyman's Library, 1992), sections 22-3, p.11.

25 'Love Condemned'. From: Peter T. Ricketts (ed. and tr.), *Le Breviari d'Amor de Matfre Ermengaud* (Leiden, Brill, 1976), p.42.

26 'Love of Christ'. From: B. A. Windeatt (tr.), *The Book of Margery Kempe* (Harmondsworth, Penguin, 1985), chapter 28, pp.105-6.

26 'Love of God'. From: Suzanne Noffke (tr.), *The Letters of Catherine of Siena*, Medieval and Renaissance Texts and Studies Series vol.52 (State University of New York at Binghampton, 1988), vol.1, letter 23, pp.87-90.

28 'Astrology'. From: Anna Komnene, *The Alexiad*, tr. Elizabeth A. S. Dawes (London, Routledge and Kegan Paul, 1928, repr. 1967), book VI, pp.148-9.

29 'Misfortune'. From: T. Carmi (ed.), *The Penguin Book of Hebrew Verse* (Harmondsworth, Penguin, 1981), p.353.

30 'Fortune'. From: Geoffroi de Charny, *The Book of Chivalry*, tr. R. W. Kaeuper and E. Kennedy (Philadelphia, University of Pennsylvania Press, 1996), sections 23-4, pp.131-3.

31 'A Teacher's Warning' From: Robert Browning, 'The correspondence of a tenth century Byzantine scholar', *Byzantion*, 24 (1954), pp.397-452 [repr. in Robert Browning, *Studies* (Aldershot, Ashgate Publishing, 1977)].

31 'Children'. From: Juan de Mata Carriazo (ed.), *Hechos del condestable Don Miguel Lusas de Iranzo (crónico del siglo)* (Madrid, Espasa-Calpe SA, 1940) ; tr. T. Ruíz.

32 'The Miracle of the Blind Boy'. From: Pamela Sheingorn (tr.), *The Book of Sainte Foy* (Philadelphia, University of Pennsylvania Press, 1995), Miracles, 3:7, pp.183-5.

33 'The Calendar'. From: Anon. 'The Chronicle of 754' in Kenneth Baxter Wolf (tr.), *Conquerors and Chroniclers of Early Medieval Spain* (Liverpool University Press, 1990), para.95, pp.156-8.

34 'The White Cat'. From: Eileen Power (ed.), *Poems from the Irish*, tr. Robin Flower (London, Benn, 1926).

35 'An Arranged Marriage'. From: John Wortley (tr.), *The Spiritually Beneficial Tales of Paul, Bishop of Monembasia* (Kalamazoo, MI, Cistercian Publications, 1996), number 12/II, pp.104-5.

36 'Advice to an Officer'. From: B. Wassilievsky and V. Jernstedt (eds.), *Cecaumeni Strategicon* (Imperial University of St Petersburg, 1896), p.19; (repr. Amsterdam, Hakkert, 1965) tr. C. M. Roueché.

37 'Dress'. From: George Nedungatt and Michael Featherstone (eds.), *The Council in Trullo Revisited* (Rome, Pontificio Istituto Orientale, 1995), canon 45, pp.126-8.

39 'The Gift of a Book'. From: Morris Bishop (tr.), *Letters from Petrarch* (Bloomington, Indiana University Press, 1966), book XV, pp.291-2.

40 'A New Fair'. From: R. Vaughan (ed. and tr.), *The Chronicles of Matthew Paris: Monastic Life in the 13th Century* (New York, St Martin's Press/Gloucester, Alan Sutton, 1984), p.149.

41 'Rag Day'. From: David Parlett (tr.), *Selections from the Carmina Burana. A new verse translation* (Harmondsworth, Penguin, 1986), p.172.

43 'Dress Sense'. From: Geoffroi de Charny, *The Book of Chivalry*, tr. R. W. Kaeuper and E. Kennedy (Philadelphia, University of Pennsylvania Press, 1996), sections 42.216-20, 43.1-10, 43.24-42, pp. 191-3.

44 'A Scarlet Dress'. From: Chaucer, *The Canterbury Tales. The Wife of Bath's Prologue*, tr. Nevill Coghill (Harmondsworth, Penguin, 1951), pp.272-3.

46 'A Wedding Feast'. From: Juan de Mata Carriazo (ed.), *Crónica del Halconero de Juan II*, Pedro Carillo de Huerte (Madrid, Espasa-Calpe, 1946), pp.565-6. Teofilo Ruíz (tr.)

47 'Warships'. From: Simon Keynes and Michael Lapidge (trs.), *Alfred the Great, Asser's Life of Alfred and Other Contemporary Sources* (Harmondsworth, Penguin, 1983), pp.118-19.

48 'Warfare'. From: Michael Kritovoulos, *History of Mehmed the Conqueror*, tr. Charles T. Riggs (Princeton University Press, 1954), pp.66-77.

50 'Building'. From: Erwin Panofsky (ed. and tr.), *Abbot Suger on the Abbey Church of St Denis and its Art Treasures* (Princeton University Press, 1946, repr. 1979).

51 'Travel Documents'. From: S. D. Goitein (tr.). *Letters of Medieval Jewish Traders* (Princeton University Press, 1973), p.339.

52 'A Shepherd's Duty'. From: D. Oschinsky (ed. and tr.), *Walter of Henley and Other Treatises on Estate Management and Accounting* (Oxford, Clarendon Press, 1971), p.287. Reprinted by permission of the publishers.

53 'Magic'. From: John Osborne (tr.), *Master Gregorius: The Marvels of Rome* (Toronto, Pontifical Institute of Medieval Studies, 1987), pp.17, 24.

54 'The Miracle of the Testicles'. From: V. Crisafulli and J. Nesbitt (trs.), *The Miracles of Artemios* no. 21 (Leiden, Brill, 1997), p.125-31.

56 'Trading in India'. From: Ronald Latham (tr.), *The Travels of Marco Polo* (Harmondsworth, Penguin, 1958), pp.290-2.

58 'After Dinner Entertainment'. From: Liutprand of Cremona, *Antapodosis. Tit-for-Tat*, tr. F. Wright (London, Routledge, 1930), book 6, chapter 9, p.155. [repr. London, J. M. Dent/Everyman, 1993].

60 'On the Need for Discretion'. From: M. E. Cosenza (ed.), *Petrarch, the Revolution of Cola di Rienzo*, 2nd edn (New York, Italica Press, 1986), p.54-6.

61 'War Personified'. From: T. Carmi (ed.), *The Penguin Book of Hebrew Verse* (Harmondsworth, Penguin, 1981), p.291.

62 'Summer Storms'. From: T. Reuter (tr.), *The Annals of Fulda* (Manchester University Press, 1992), p.63.

63 'Ugly Feet'. From: Snorri Sturluson, *From the Sagas of the Norse Kings*, tr. Erling Monson and A. H. Smith (Oslo, Dreyers Forlag, 1973).

64 'Summer Love'. From: Marcelle Thiébaux, *The Writings of Medieval Women. An Anthology*, 2nd edn (New York, Garland, 1994), pp.284-6.

66 'Heat'. From: Froissart, *Chronicles*, tr. Geoffrey Brereton (Harmondsworth, Penguin, 1968), book 3, pp.328-34.

68 'Harvest'. From: Walter Ashburner (ed. and tr.), 'The Farmer's Law', *Journal of Hellenic Studies*, 30 (1910), pp.92-4 [translation modified by Judith Herrin].

69 'Hunger'. From: William Langland, *Piers the Plowman*, ed. and tr.

J. F. Goodridge (Harmondsworth, Penguin, 1959), book VI, lines 282f, p.127.

70 'Monks Reaping'. From: John Moschos, *The Spiritual Meadow*, tr. John Wortley, Cistercian Studies Series no. 139 (Kalamazoo, MI, Cistercian Publications, 1992), pp.152-3.

71 'Hiring Reapers'. From: D. Oschinsky (ed. and tr.), *Walter of Henley and Other Treatises on Estate Management and Accounting* (Oxford, Clarendon Press, 1971), p.445. Reprinted by permission of the publishers.

72 'Prayer Before an Ordeal'. From: Oliver J. Thatched and E. H. MacNeal, *A Source Book for Medieval History* (New York, Charles Scribner's Sons, 1905), pp.404-6.

73 'Prayer'. From: Symeon of Thessaloniki, *Treatise on Prayer*, tr. H. L. N. Simmons (Brookline, MA, Hellenic College Press, 1984), chapter 4, pp.14-15.

74 'Health'. From: Platina, *On Right Pleasure and Good Health*, ed. and tr. Mary Ellen Milham, Medieval and Renaissance Texts and Studies Series vol.168 (Tempe, AZ, Rennaissance Society of America 1998), vol.17, p.155.

75 'Threshing'. From: 'The Life of St Theodore of Sykeon' in E. A. Dawes and N. H. Baynes (trs.), *Three Byzantine Saints* (Crestwood, St Vladimir's Seminary Press, 1977, originally published 1948), section 114, pp.162-3.

76 'Warfare'. From: T. Reuter (tr.), *The Annals of Fulda* (Manchester University Press, 1992), p.105.

77 'Disguise'. From: Froissart, *Chronicles*, tr. Geoffrey Brereton (Harmondsworth, Penguin, 1968), book 2, pp.238-40.

78 'Fiesta'. From: Juan de Mata Carriazo (ed.), *Hechos del condestable Don Miguel Lucas de Iranzo (crónico del siglo XV)* (Madrid, Espasa-Calpe, 1940), chapter XVI, pp.164-6; tr. T. Ruíz.

79 'The Trial of Joan of Arc'. From: *The trial of Joan of Arc, 27 March 1431*. [A verbatim report of the proceedings from the Orleans manuscript, tr. W. S. Scott (London, Folio Society, 1956), p.134-5.

80 'Ceremony of Marriage'. From: C. W. Grocock (tr.), *The Ruodlieb* (Warminster, Aris and Phillips, 1985), section XIV, lines 18-90.

81 'Jews of Babylonia'. From: Manuel Komroff (ed.), *Contemporaries of Marco Polo* (London, Jonathan Cape, 1928), pp.286-92.

82 'Marriage'. From: Marcelle Thiébaux, *The Writings of Medieval Women. An Anthology*, 2nd edn (New York, Garland, 1994), pp.260-1.

85 'An Artist's Vision'. From: Gordon Whatley (ed. and tr.), *The Saint of London, the Life and Miracles of St Erkenwald*, Medieval and Renaissance Texts and Studies Series, vol.58 (State University of New York at Binghampton, 1989), pp.159-61.

86 'Artistic Techniques'. From: Theophilus, *On Various Arts*, tr. C. R. Dodwell (London, Thomas Nelson and Sons, 1961), intro. 3-4, sections 46-9.

90 'The Elephant'. From: Anon. *Entertaining Tales of Quadrupeds*, ed. Vasiliki Tsiouni (Munich, Institut für Byzantinistik und Neugriechische Philogie der Universität München, 1972), sections 26-7; tr. George Baloglou and Nick Nicholas in collaboration with Tassos Karanastasis – work in progress.

92 'The Cock and the Wolf'. From: Jan M. Ziolkowski, *Talking Animals. Medieval Latin Beast Poetry, 750–1150* (Philadelphia, University of Pennsylvania Press, 1993), p.241.

93 'Prayer'. From: W. Bader (ed.), *St Francis at Prayer*, tr. A. Neame (London, Darton, Longman and Todd, 1988), p.62.

93 'A Miraculous Statue'. From: John Osborne (tr.), *Master Gregorius: The Marvels of Rome* (Toronto, Pontifical Institute of Medieval Studies, 1987), no.9, p.25.

94 'Pilgrimage'. From: William Melczar (tr.), *The Pilgrim's Guide to Santiago de Compostela* (New York, Italica Press, 1993), pp.91-3.

95 'Travel'. From: Manuel Komroff (ed.), *Contemporaries of Marco Polo* (London, Jonathan Cape, 1928), pp.286-92.

96 'The Swan'. From: Hugh of Fouilloy, *The Medieval Book of Birds*, Willene B. Clark (ed. and tr.), Medieval and Renaissance Texts and Studies Series (State University of New York at Binghampton, 1992), chapter 58.

99 'Ambassadors'. From: Liutprand of Cremona, *Antapodosis. Tit-for-Tat*, tr. F. Wright (London, Routledge, 1930), book 6, chapter 4, pp.152-3. [repr. London, J. M. Dent/Everyman, 1993].

100 'Prayer for a Soul in Purgatory'. From: Jacobus de Voragine, *The Golden Legend*, tr. Granger Ryan and Helmut Ripperger (London, Longman, 1948), p.650.

102 'The Feast of St Demetrios'. From: Barry Baldwin (tr.), *Timarion* (Detroit, Wayne State University Press, 1984), pp.43-5.

104 'A Cunning Escape'. From: Anna Komnene, *The Alexiad*, tr. Elizabeth A. S. Dawes (London, Routledge and Kegan Paul, 1928, repr. 1967), book XI, pp.297-8.

107 'Fiesta'. From: an old German proverb *'Kein Spiel ohne Narren'*.

107 'The Autumn of Life'. From: E. J. Martin (ed.), *Twenty-One Medieval Latin Poems* (London, Scholartis Press, 1931), p.109.

108 'Autumn'. From: T. Carmi (ed.), *The Penguin Book of Hebrew Verse* (Harmondsworth, Penguin, 1981), p.241.

109 'The Miracle of the Bloody Shirt'. From: Janet L. Nelson (tr.), *The Annals of St-Bertin* (Manchester University Press, 1991), p.101.

111 'Jerusalem Fair'. From: Adamnan, *De locis sanctis*, ed. and tr. Denis Meehan, Scriptores Latini Hiberniae vol.3 (Dublin Institute of Advanced Studies, 1958), pp.41-3.

112 'Pagans'. From: Liutprand of Cremona, *Antapodosis. Tit-for-Tat*, tr. F. Wright (London, Routledge, 1930), book 2, sections 25-31, pp.48-51 [rep. London, J.M. Dent/Everyman, 1993].

114 'The Effects of Wine'. From: Juan Ruiz, *The Book of Good Love*, tr. Elisha Kent Kane, intro. by John Esten Keller (Chapel Hill, University of North Carolina Press, 1968), verse 544-5, p.82.

114 'A Warning Against Wine'. From: *Pseudo-Bede Collectanea*, ed. J.-P. Migne, Patrologia Latina vol.94 (Paris, 1850), tr. Judith Herrin.

115 'An Auspicious Birth'. From: H. E. Butler (ed. and tr.), *The Autobiography of Giraldus Cambrensis* (London, Jonathan Cape, 1937), pp.37-8.

116 'A Portent of Death'. From: George Akropolites, *Chronicle*, ed. A Heisenberg (Leipzig, Teubner, 1889), para.39, pp.62-4; tr. Judith Herrin and Charlotte Roueché.

119 'Crusading in the West'. From: Louise and Jonathan Riley-Smith (trs.), *The Crusades: Idea and Reality, 1095–1274* (London, Edward Arnold, 1981), p.40.

120 'Crusading in the East'. From: A. C. Krey, *The First Crusade: Accounts of Eye-Witnesses and Participants* (Princeton University Press, 1921), pp.161-2.

122 'Hunting'. From: Guillaume de Machaut, *The Tale of the Alerion*, ed. and tr. Minnette Gaudet and Constance B. Hieatt (University of Toronto Press, 1994), part 1, lines 863-1089, 1197-1210.

124 'Disruption of Trade'. From: S. D. Goitein (tr.), *Letters of Medieval Jewish Traders* (Princeton University Press, 1973), pp.245-6.

125 'The Old Nun'. From: A.-M. Talbot (ed. and tr.), *Holy Women of Byzantium* (Washington DC, Dumbarton Oaks, 1996), chapters 37-8, pp.195-7.

127 'A Miraculous Cure of Depression'. From: Pamela Sheingorn (tr.), *The Book of Sainte Foy* (Philadelphia, University of Pennsylvania Press, 1995), Miracles, 3:7, p.152-4.

129 'Pleasure Gardens'. From: Procopius, *On Buildings*, tr. H. B. Dewing (Cambridge, MA/London, Harvard University Press, 1961), vol.7, pp.87-91. Reprinted by permission of the publishers and the Loeb Classical Library.

130 'Relics'. From: Adamnan, *De locis sanctis*, ed. and tr. Denis Meehan, *Scriptores Latini Hiberniae* (Dublin Institute of Advanced Studies, 1958), vol.3, pp.53-5.

132 'Relics of the Saints'. From: William Melczar (tr.), *The Pilgrim's Guide to Santiago de Compostela* (New York, Italica Press, 1993), pp.96-7.

134 'Old Age'. From: B. A. Windeatt (tr.), *The Book of Margery Kempe* (Harmondsworth, Penguin, 1985), chapter 76, pp.219-21.

135 'Inquisition'. From: Jean-Claude Schmitt, *The Holy Greyhound. Guinefort, Healer of Children since the Thirteenth Century*, tr. Martin Thom (Cambridge University Press, 1983), pp.4-6.

136 'The Black Death". From: Giovanni Bocccaccio, *The Decameron*, Mark Muska and Peter Bondanella (trs.) (New York, W. W. Norton and Co, 1982), pp.6-12. Reprinted by permission of the publishers.

138 'Coping with Plague'. From: John Henderson, 'The Black Death in Florence: medieval and communal responses' in Steven Bassett (ed.), *Death in Towns. Urban Responses to the Dying and the Dead, 100–1600* (Leicester University Press, 1992), p.138.

139 'The Epitaph of Harald'. From: Lis Jacobsen and Erik Moltke, *Danmarks runeindskrifter* (Copenhagen, Ejnar Munksgaards Forlag, 1941–2); tr. K. H. Holman.

140 'A Miraculous Icon'. From: Alice-Mary Talbot, 'Epigrams of Manuel Philes on the Theotokos tes Peges and its Art', *Dumbarton Oaks Papers*, 48 (1994), p.153.

140 'Birth'. From: Paul J. Archambault (tr.), *A Monk's Confession. The Memoirs of Guibert of Nogent* (University Park, PA, Penn State University Press, 1996), pp.10-11.

142 'Restriction of Prostitution'. From: Emilie Amt (ed.), *Women's Lives in Medieval Europe. A Sourcebook* (London/New York, Routledge, Chapman and Hall, 1993), pp.210, 212.

143 'Reform of Prostitution'. From: E. R. A. Sewter (tr.), *Fourteen Byzantine Rulers. The Chronographia of Michael Psellus* (Harmondsworth, Penguin, 1966), p.108.

145 'Ballade'. From: Dante, *New Life*, tr. Dino S. Cervigni and Edward Vasta (University of Notre Dame Press, 1995), pp.65-7.

146 'An Accusation of Rape'. From: Froissart, *Chronicles*, tr. Geoffrey Brereton (Harmondsworth, Penguin, 1968), book 3, pp.309-11.

148 'Trial by Combat'. From: Froissart, *Chronicles*, tr. Geoffrey Brereton (Harmondsworth, Penguin, 1968), book 3, pp.313-14.

150 'Swimming'. From: Einhard, *The Life of Charlemagne*, tr. Lewis Thorpe (Harmondsworth, Penguin, 1969), pp.76-7.

152 'Rape'. From: Christine de Pizan, *The Book of the City of Ladies*, tr. Earl Jeffrey Richards (London, Pan Books, 1983), chapters 44-6, pp.160-4.

154 'Winter'. From: Cyril Mango and Roger Scott (trs. and eds.), *The Chronicle of Theophanes Confessor* (Oxford, Clarendon Press, 1997), pp.600-1. Reprinted by permission of the publishers.

155 'An Orphaned Child'. From: John Wortley (tr.), *The Spiritually Beneficial Tales of Paul, Bishop of Monembasia* (Kalamazoo, MI, Cistercian Publications, 1996), 8/III, pp.86-8.

157 'Piracy'. From: Ronald Latham (tr.), *The Travels of Marco Polo* (Harmondsworth, Penguin, 1958), pp.290-1.

158 'Dangerous Games'. From:

159 'Music'. From: 'The Romance of Horn' in Judith Weiss (tr.), *The Birth of Romance* (London, Everyman's Library, 1992), section 137, pp.65-6.

160 'Courtship'. From: 'The Romance of Horn' in Judith Weiss (tr.), *The Birth of Romance* (London, Everyman's Library, 1992), sections 132-4, pp.63-4.

161 'A Game of Chess'. From: C. W. Grocock (ed. and tr.), *The Ruodlieb* (Warminster, Aris and Phillips, 1985), pp.59-61.

162 'Normans'. From: Dorothy Whitelock, David Douglas and Susie Tucker (revs., trs. and eds.), *The Anglo-Saxon Chronicle* (London, Eyre and Spottiswoode, 1961), version D, pp.142-5.

163 'A Race'. From: 'The Saga of Sigurd the Crusader' in Snorri Sturluson, *From the Sagas of the Norse Kings*, tr. Erling Monson and A. H. Smith (Oslo, Dreyers Forlag, 1973), pp.373-4.

164 'A Boar Hunt'. From: Brian Stone (tr.), *Sir Gawain and the Green Knight*, 2nd edn (Harmondsworth, Penguin, 1974), pp.74-81.

167 'Teaching'. From: Gordon Whatley (ed. and tr.), *The Saint of London, the Life and Miracles of St Erkenwald*, Medieval and Renaissance Texts and Studies Series vol.58 (State University of New York at Binghampton, 1989).

169 'Dance'. From: Guglielmo Ebreo of Pesaro, *On the Practice or Art of Dancing*, ed. and tr. Barbara Sparti (Oxford, Clarendon Press, 1993), pp.93, 109-10, 233. Reprinted by permission of the publishers.

170 'Dance Song'. From: Marcelle Thiébaux, *The Writings of Medieval Women. An Anthology*, 2nd edn (New York, Garland, 1994), pp.565-6.

173 'Entertainments'. From: Juan de Mata Carriazo (ed.), *Crónica del Halconero de Juan II, Pedro Carillo de Huerte* (Madrid, Espasa-Calpe, 1946) pp.565-6. Teofilo Ruíz (tr.)

174 'The Pleasures of Music'. From: Guglielmo Ebreo of Pesaro, *On the Practice or Art of Dancing*, ed. and tr. Barbara Sparti (Oxford, Clarendon Press, 1993), pp.88-9. Reprinted by permission of the publishers.

176 'Prayer to the Virgin'. From: Sister Benedicta Ward (tr.), *The Prayers and Meditations of Saint Anselm* (Harmondsworth, Penguin, 1973), p.107.

179 'Christmas'. From: Brian Stone (tr.), *Sir Gawain and the Green Knight*, 2nd edn (Harmondsworth, Penguin, 1974), sections 3-4, pp.22-4.

180 'Snow'. From: T. Reuter (tr.), *The Annals of Fulda* (Manchester University Press, 1992), p.73.

182 'The Virgin's Complaint'. From: T. Carmi (ed.), *The Penguin Book of Hebrew Verse* (Harmondsworth, Penguin, 1981), p.424.

182 'Poverty'. From: Ingrid Sanness Johnsen, *Norges innskrifter med de yngre runer*, ed. Aslak Liestl and James E. Knirk (Oslo, Norsk Historisk Kjeldeskrift–Institutt, 1990); tr. K. H. Holman.

186 'The Will of Alfred'. From: Simon Keynes and Michael Lapidge (trs.), *Alfred the Great, Asser's Life of Alfred and Other Contemporary Sources* (Harmondsworth, Penguin, 1983), pp.174-8.

187 'The Death of Guillaume Champlitte'. From: H. E. Lurier (tr.), *Crusaders as Conquerors. The Chronicle of Morea* (New York, Columbia University Press, 1964), lines 7770-820.

189 'Riches'. From: C. W. R. D. Moseley (tr.), *The Travels of Sir John Mandeville* (Harmondsworth, Penguin, 1983), sections 23, 25, pp.242, 253.

190 'Travel'. From: George T. Dennis (tr.), *The Letters of Manuel II Palaiologus* (Washington DC, Dumbarton Oaks, 1977), letter 38, pp.100-2.

191 'A Byzantine Emperor Abroad'. From: E. M. Thompson (tr.), *The*

Chronicle of Adam of Usk, AD 1377–1421, 2nd edn (Oxford University Press, 1904), p.220. Reprinted by permission of the publishers.

192 'Death'. From: Michael Psellus, 'A Funeral Oration', tr. M. J. Kyriakis in 'Medieval European Society as seen in two eleventh century texts of Michael Psellus', *Byzantine Studies/Etudes Byzantines*, 3/2 (1976), pp.92-8.

195 'Burial'. From: R. Vaughan (ed. and tr.), *The Chronicles of Matthew Paris: Monastic Life in the 13th Century* (New York, St Martin's Press/Gloucester, Alan Sutton, 1984), pp.63-4.

196 'A Byzantine View of Crusaders'. From: Harry Magoulias (tr.), *O City of Byzantium, The Annals of Niketas Choniates* (Detroit, Wayne State University Press, 1984), pp.323-5.

199 'Easter Regulations'. From: George Nedungatt and Michael Featherstone (eds.), *The Council in Trullo Revisited* (Rome, Pontificio Istituto Orientale, 1995), canon 66, pp.148-9.

199 'Calculating the Date of Easter'. From: Bertram Colgrave and R. A. B. Mynors (eds.), *Bede's Ecclesiastical History of the English People* (Oxford, Clarendon Press, 1969). Reprinted by permission of the publishers.

200 'Easter in Jerusalem'. From: Aubrey Stewart (tr.), *Theoderich, Guide to the Holy Land* (New York, Italica Press, 1986), pp.14-15.

Index of Manuscripts

BL   The British Library, London, England.
BNF Bibliothèque nationale de France, Paris.
BP   Biblioteca Palatina, Parma, Italy.
FAS Fundaçion Amigos de Sefarad, facsimile edition of the Alba Bible, Palaçio de Liria, Madrid, Spain.
IM   The Israel Museum, Jerusalem, Rothschild Miscellany

Captioned images are listed against the appropriate Roman numeral. Uncaptioned images are listed without numbering. Page numbers refer to the page on which the text *starts*.

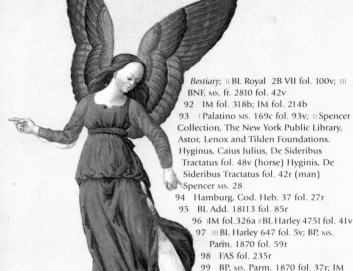

Bestiary; II BL Royal 2B VII fol. 100v; III BNF, MS. fr. 2810 fol. 42v

92 IM fol. 318b; IM fol. 214b

93 I Palatino MS. 169c fol. 93v; II Spencer Collection, The New York Public Library, Astor, Lenox and Tilden Foundations. Hyginus, Caius Julius, De Sideribus Tractatus fol. 48v (horse) Hyginis, De Sideribus Tractatus fol. 42r (man) Spencer MS. 28

94 Hamburg, Cod. Heb. 37 fol. 27r

95 BL Add. 18113 fol. 85r

96 IM fol.326a II BL Harley 4751 fol. 41v

97 III BL Harley 647 fol. 5v; BP, MS. Parm. 1870 fol. 59r

98 FAS fol. 235r

99 BP, MS. Parm. 1870 fol. 37r; IM fol. 174b

100 FAS fol. 467v; BP, MS. Parm. 1870 ff. 189v, 82v

102 I Pliny AL.1504-1896 Courtesy of the Trustees of the V&A, London V&A Picture Library; IM fol. 134b

103 II Benaki Museum, Athens Ms 2976 fol. 14v

104 FAS fol. 48r

105 I BNF, Fr. 2810 fol. 107; II BNF, Esp.30 ff. 2v-6r

106 I BL Add.28162 fol. 10v

107 II IM fol. 355b; III IM fol. 302a; IV IM fol. 352a

108 I Osterreichische Nationalbibliothek Ms Series Nova 2644 fol. 54v; FAS fol. 188r

109 II Osterreichische Nationalbibliothek Ms Series Nova 2644 fol. 105v; FAS fol. 188r

111 BL Add. 28681 fol. 9v; BL Add. 14761 fol. 40

113 I FAS fol. 476v; II FAS fol. 173v; BP, MS. Parm. 1870 fol. 79v

114 I IM fol. 125b; II IM fol. 131a; BP, MS. Parm. 1870 fol. 89a; BL, MS. Add 14761 fol. 26v

115 III BNF, MS. fr. 2810 fol. 36; BP, MS. Parm. 1870 fol. 100r

116 I BL Roy. 6.E.VI fol. 16; II BL Add.39943 fol. 74v; IM ff. 134b, 147b

119 I FAS fol. 341v; II BNF, Ms fr. 2810 fol. 232; BL Add 14761 fol. 57r

120 FAS fol. 225v

122 I BP Pliny 214; II IM fol. 328a; III IM fol. 403a

124 I Pliny Book XIII Courtesy of the Trustees of the V&A; II IM fol. 270a; III FAS fol. 187bv

127 I Osterreichische Nationalbibliothek Cod. 2759 fol. 174v; BP, MS. Parm. 1870 fol. 38r

129 I BL Harl. 603 fol. 54v; II BNF, MS. fr. Latin I fol.243; BP, MS. Parm. 1870 fol. 15r

130 I BNF Latin 8850 fol. 180v; II BNF MS. Grec 139 fol. 435v

132 I The Pierpont Morgan Library/Art Resource, NY M.736, fol. 20v; BP, MS. Parm. 1870 fol. 118v

134 I BL MS. Sloane 278 fol. 34v; II IM fol. 335b

135 I BL MS. Sloane 278 fol. 54v; II BL, MS. Add 14761 fol. 160r

136 I FAS fol. 227v; II FAS fol. 339v; III FAS fol. 211v; BP Parm. 3289

138 I BL Roy.6.E.VI fol. 301 ; II BL Harley 4751 fol. 40; III BL Cott.Tib.B.V. fol. 40v; IV FAS f. 247v

140 I FAS fol. 28r; II Wellcome Institute Library, London WMS 544 fol. 65r

142 I Courtesy of Ministero per I Beni e le Attivita Culturali Biblioteca Casanatense, Rome. MS 4182 fol. CXCVI;

143 II BNF, MS. fr Arsenal 5196 fol. 372

145 I BP, MS. Parm. 1870 fol. 213v; II Österreichische National-bibliothek Cod. 2617 fol. 53r; BP, MS. Parm. 1870 fol. 184r

146 I BNF, MS. fr. 24541 fol. 93; II BNF, MS. fr. 1586 fol. 23

148 I IM fol. 147a; II BL Harl.4379 fol. 23v

150 I IM fol. 90a; II BP Palatino 236 (1-4); BP, MS. Parm. 1870 fol. 181v

152 I FAS fol. 181v; II FAS fol. 224v; FAS fol. 292r

154 I Biblioteca Nazionale Marciana, Venice Gr. Z. 479 fol. 59r; BP, MS. Parm. 1870 fol. 92v

155 II BL Sloane 249 fol. 197 (top); BL Sloane 2463 fol. 218v (bottom); BL, MS. Add 14761 fol. 34v

157 I BNF MS. fr. 2810 fol. 188; II BNF, MS. fr. 2810 fol. 73v, III BP, MS. Parm. 1870 fol. 198r;

158 I BP Palatino 56 C115v; II BL Harl.4375 fol. 151v

159 I BL, MS. Add 14761 fol. 61r; BL Harl.4375 fol. 151v

160 I Universitätsbibliothek Heidelberg Cod.pal.Germ.848, fol. 311r; BP, MS. Parm. 1870 43r

161 I BL Add.16561 fol. 36v; BP, MS. Parm. 1870 fol. 24v

162 FAS fol. 327v

163 BL Royal.12. FXIII fol. 42v; BL Add 14761 fol. 57r

164 I BL Cott. Nero AX fol. 129; II BL Egerton 1146 fol. 13v; III BL Harl. 3244 fol. 47; BL Add 14761 ff. 64v, 57r

167 I BL Royal.20 D.IV. fol. 207; II St Paul's School Library

169 Dean and Chapter of Winchester (photo:Miki Slingsby) Winchester Bible fol. 270v, c1160; BP, MS. Parm. 1870 fol. 105r

170 I BL. Sloane 2435 fol.8v; II BP, MS. Parm. 1870 fol. 41v; III Bodleian Library, Oxford Ms. Douce 331 fol. 26r

173 I Valencia, Biblioteca Universitaria BUV, Ms 837; BP, MS. Parm. 1870 ff. 82v, 89r

174 I IM fol. 246b; II BL Add. 24098 fol. 19v; IM fol. 235a

176 I The J. Paul Getty Museum, Los Angeles MS. Ludwig VI.6 fol. 2; II The Board of Trinity College Dublin, Book of Kells TCD MS 58 fol. 200r

179 I BNF MS. fr. arsénal 5072 fol. 270v; II BL Arundel 83 fol. 124

180 I BL, Harl. 4751, fol. 27r; II BL, Add 5686 fol. 60r

182 I FAS 218r; II BL Add. 24189 fol. 15r; BL, MS. Add 14761 fol. 24r; BL, MS. Add 14761 fol. 20v

184 Kungl.biblioteket (The Royal Library) Stockholm A135 fol. 9v-11r

186 I BL Cott.Tib.B.I fol. 132; BL, MS. Add 14761 fol. 24v; II Kungl.biblioteket (The Royal Library) Stockholm A135 fol. 9v-11r

187 I Basilika St.Godehard, Hildesheim St. Alban's Psalter fol. 48; II Ms Palatino GR5

189 I BNF, MS. fr. 2810 fol. 40; II BNF, MS. fr. 2810 fol. 137v; III IM fol. 324b; IV IM fol. 328b

190 I IM fol. 339b; II IM fol. 334b

191 BNF MS. fr. 2810 fol.3; BL add 14761 fol. 64v

192 I BL Add. 50002 fol. 85r; IM fol. 342a; IM 460a

195 I BL Harl. 4425 fol. 59; IM fol. 274b

196 I Sir Paul Getty, K.B.E. - Wormsley Library/BL loan 88 fol. 1b; II FAS fol. 128r; III FAS fol. 127v

199 The Board of Trinity College Dublin Book of Kells TCD MS 58 27v

200 I BL C.14.c.13, II BL Add 22635 fol.44

202 BP, MS. Parm. 1870 fol. 65v

207 BL, Add 22413 fol. 71r

208 BL, Roy.20.C.VII. fol. 41v

Manuscript Bibliography

Alexander J. J. G. *The Painted Page, Italian Renaissance Book Illumination 1450-1550*, Royal Academy of Arts, London and Prestel Verlag, Munich 1994

Andronicos M., *The Greek Museums* Ekdotike Athenon S.A., Athens 1975

Avril F., *Manuscript Painting at the Court of France*, George Braziller, New York 1978

Avrin L., *Scribes, Script & Books*, American Library Association/The British Library, London 1991

Avrin L., Sirat C., *Micrography as Art* , Centre National de la Recherche Scientifique, Paris 1981

Backhouse J., *Book of Hours*, The British Library, London 1985

Backhouse J., *The Bedford Hours*, The British Library, London 1990

Backhouse J., *The Lindisfarne Gospels*, Phaidon, Oxford 1981

Barnavi E., *A Historical Atlas of The Jewish People*, Hutchinson, London 1992

Basing P., *Trades and Crafts in Medieval Manuscripts*, The British Library, London 1990

Beit-Arié M., Cohen E., Loewe R., Rowland-Smith D., Schmelzer M., Snir Y., *The Barcelona Haggadah*, Facsimile Editions, London 1992

Beit-Arié M., Fishof I., Foot M., Mortara-Ottolenghi L., Simonsohn S., Ta-Shema I., *The Rothschild Miscellany*, Facsimile Editions, London 1989

Beit-Arié M., Metzger T., Silver E., *The Parma Psalter*, Facsimile Editions, London 1996

Bologna G., *Illuminated Manuscripts, The Book Before Gutenberg*, Weidenfeld and Nicolson, New York 1988

Brown M. P., *Anglo-Saxon Manuscripts*, The British Library, London 1991

Brown M., *Understanding Illuminated Manuscripts, A Guide To Technical Terms*, The British Library, London 1994

Brown P., *The Book of Kells*, Thames & Hudson, London 1980

Carmi T., *The Penguin Book of Hebrew Verse*, Penguin Books USA 1981

Churchill W., *The Island Race*, Webb & Bower, Exeter 1985

Cogliati Arano L., *The Medieval Health Handbook*, George Braziller, New York 1976

de Hamel C., *A History of Illuminated Manuscripts*, Phaidon Press, Oxford 1986

Deák G., *Treasures from the New York Public Library*, Astor Lenox and Tilden Foundations, New York 1985

Donovan C., *The Winchester Bible*, The British Library/Winchester Cathedral, London 1993

Garel M., *D'Une Main Forte*, Bibliothèque Nationale, Paris 1991

Glenisson J., *Le Livre Au Moyen Age*, Presses du CNRS, France 1988

Goldstein D., *The Jewish Poets of Spain*, Penguin Books, London 1971

Gullick M., *Calligraphy*, Studio Editions, London 1990

Gutman J., *Hebrew Manuscript Painting*, Chatto & Windus, London 1979

Harvey P. D. A., *Medieval Maps*, The British Library, London 1991

Hatchwell Toledano M., Ben-Ami S., Fellous-Rozenblat S., Keller A., Lazar M., MacKay A., Schonfield J., *The Alba Bible*, Fundacion Amigos de Sefarad, Madrid / Facsimile Editions, London 1992

Jones P. M., *Medieval Medicine in Illuminated Manuscripts*, The British Library, London 1984

Kedoourie E., *The Jewish World Revelation Prophecy and History*, Thames & Hudson, London 1979

Kelliher H., Brown S., *English Literary Manuscripts*, The British Library, London 1986

Loewe R., *The Rylands Haggadah, A Medieval Sephardi Masterpiece in Facsimile*, Thames & Hudson, London 1988

Mead A. H., *A Miraculous Draught of Fishes, A History of St Paul's School 1509-1990*, James & James, London 1990

Metzger T. & M., *La Vie Juive au Moyen Age*, Office du Livre S.A., Fribourg 1982

Mondadori A., *Arte e Cultura Ebraiche In Emilia-Romangna*, De Luca Edizione D'Arte S.p.A., Rome 1988

Narkiss B., *Hebrew Illuminated Manuscripts*, Keter, Jerusalem 1969

Narkiss, B., Cohen-Mushlin A., *The Kennicott Bible*, Facsimile Editions, London 1985

Pächt O., *Book Illumination in The Middle Ages*, Harvey Miller, London 1986

Payne A., *Medieval Beasts*, The British Library, London 1990

Payne A., *Views of the Past*, The British Library, London 1987

Posner R., Ta-Shema I., *The Hebrew Book An Historical Survey*, Keter, Jerusalem 1975

Prescott A., *English Historical Documents*, The British Library, London 1988

Ricci F. M., *FMR International*, Franco Maria Ricci Editore Sp.A., Milan, July 1984

Searle A., *Music Manuscripts*, The British Library, London 1987

Sed-Rajna G., *The Hebrew Bible In Medieval Illuminated Manuscripts*, Rizzoli, New York 1987

Tamani G., *Il Canon medicinae di Avicenna nella tradizione ebraica*, Studio Editoriale Programma, Padova 1988

Thomas A., *Great Books and Book Collectors*, Weidenfeld and Nicolson, London 1975

Thomas M., *The Golden Age, Manuscript Painting at the Time of Jean, Duke of Berry*, George Braziller, New York 1979

Titley N., *Persian Miniature Painting*, The British Library, London 1983

Werber E., *The Sarajevo Haggadah*, Prosveta – Beograd Svjetlost, Sarajevo 1983

Whalley J. I., *Pliny The Elder Historia Naturalis*, Victoria and Albert Museum, Oregon Press, London 1982

A Medieval Miscellany has been typset in Poliphilus and
Giovanni Book and printed in 5 colours on Gardapat 130 gsm.

First published in the United Kingdom in 1999 by Weidenfeld & Nicolson

Text copyright © Judith Herrin, 1999   Introduction © Emmanuel Le Roy Ladurie, 1999
Design and layout copyright © Facsimile Editions, 1999   Translation of Introduction © Frank Wynne, 1999

The moral right of Judith Herrin to be identified as the editor of this work has
been asserted in accordance with the Copyright, Designs and Patents Act of 1988

ISBN 0 297 82483 X

Designed by Facsimile Editions
Printed in Italy by Grafiche Milani

Weidenfeld & Nicolson Illustrated Books
The Orion Publishing Group
Wellington House
125 Strand
London WC2R 0BB

Facsimile Editions Limited
40 Hamilton Terrace
London NW8 9UJ
Telephone: 020 7286 0071
Facsimile: 020 7266 3927
www.facsimile-editions.com